THE "OLD LINE MAIL"

The "Old Line Mail"

STAGECOACH DAYS IN UPSTATE NEW YORK

Richard F. Palmer

J.H.HALL. S°

North Country Books
Box 86
LAKEMONT, N.Y. 14857

First Edition

ISBN 978-1-4930-7670-3

Printed by BOONVILLE GRAPHICS, INC., Boonville, New York

Dedication

To the memory of the "Old Line" proprietors and the legion of forgotten stagecoach drivers, agents, runners, farriers, stable boys, and tavern keepers this book is dedicated.

PROPRIETORS OF THE "OLD LINE MAIL"

Aaron Thorp, Jr., Albany

Asa Sprague, Schenectady, later of Rochester

Thorp & Sprague

Thomas Powell, Schenectady

Jason Parker, Theodore S. Faxton, John Butter-fiield, Silas D. Childs, A. Shepard — Jason Parker & Co., Utica

William Storey, Cherry Valley; S. Goodwin, Madison; Col. E. Phillips, Syracuse; Isaac Sherwood, Skaneateles; Col. John M. Sherwood (son of Isaac), Auburn; Chauncey H. Coe, Canandaigua; Orrie Adams, Rochester (Adams & Blinn); Benjamin and Samuel Barton, Lewiston; Bela D. Coe (brother of Chauncey), Buffalo (C. H. Coe & Co.).

Table of Contents

Preface

The old four-horse stagecoach came into town with the clatter of galloping horses and sounding horn. Its round body was swung on leather straps; its passengers tossed about like dice in a box.

The gallant driver pulled on the reins and the four steaming horses halted in front of the tavern. Shouting boys swinging from the "boot," at the rear of the coach where baggage was stowed, fell off in a cloud of dust.

After whirling up to the tavern stoop, the traces of the horses were unhooked and the exhausted animals were led around to the stable to their familiar stalls. The stage driver himself, donned in great-coat and buckskin gloves, strolled into the tavern with his traveled air.

He was a personage in every village which depended on his arrival for the mail and the latest news from the outside world. He was an expert reinsman whose reputation was counties wide. Gazed upon with awe by the children, he was worshipped as a sort of hero of romance, who never worked, but drove his galloping horses back and forth through a perpetual holiday.

The stable boys soon trotted out a fresh team and in a few moments the passengers reclaimed their seats. The driver mounted his seat, called the "box," slung the mail pouch underneath, sounded his bugle, and with a crack of the whip galloped off down the dusty road.

This was the stagecoach era as it existed in Upstate New York for a half-century. From 1790 to 1840 the stagecoach reigned as the supreme mode of public conveyance. And during this period the stagecoach proprietors on the great western routes aligned, or associated themselves; working in close agreement to control the road.

This syndicate, as it might be termed, was known as the "Old Line Mail" and during its existence it forced opposition after opposition off the road which attempted to gain footing.

Thorpe & Sprague controlled the Albany end of the business. Jason Parker & Co. carried on through Utica and westward, while Isaac and John M. Sherwood operated from Manlius to Canandaigua. The link to Buffalo and Niagara Falls was completed by Chauncey H. and Bela D. Coe, and others.

Stagecoaching required the utmost promptitude, vigilance and activity to keep the business moving and satisfy the demands of an impatient and exacting traveling public. It was a highly organized business employing an army of agents, station-keepers, drivers, hostlers, purchasers of horses, coaches and supplies; runners, clerks, mechanics and blacksmiths.

The "Old Line" proprietors proved themselves equal to the task. Their commanding energy in moving with regularity and order such a mass of human and animal elements was proverbial.

Consider the stage-roads and turnpikes themselves. They varied with the seasons from bad to worse. During rough seasons the roads were a terror to timid passengers, occasionally becoming impassable. Now and then the stage teams became mired in deep sloughs and passengers assisted in lifting the coach out of the mudhole at the insistence of the driver.

Long stretches through swamps were bridged on corduroy roads, formed by cutting down the adjacent timber, trimming off the branches and placing the logs side-by-side across the road.

Those who have never enjoyed traveling over miles of this sort of road, at a snail's pace, can only imagine the sensations of bumping over logs, or being thrown headlong from their seats.

Under such conditions the timid often were compelled to "stop-over" at a tavern for the night and rest until another stage came along. Such a trip from Albany to

Buffalo often required nearly a week in the very early days.

Although many hardships were encountered in traveling by stage, such a journey was not entirely void of pleasures. There were deep dark forests of towering hemlocks and pines. Here and there a little clearing appeared where a settler had built a long house, feebly attempting to cultivate the rutted soil.

The scenery was varied and interesting. The passengers were sociable, and many a warm and lasting friendship was formed in the old coach. Such was the way things were before the railroads.

By 1809 the only main road across New York State was what is primarily today
Route 5. The road from Bath to Lake Erie was nothing more than a proposal.

Chapter 1

Wilderness Road to Turnpike

The pioneers came from New England by the scores to settle this new land in Upstate New York then known as the "western country." The Great Genesee Road running from Whitestown (Utica) to Geneva and beyond was thronged with rich and poor alike, all seeking a better life.

It was the year 1797 and the country was being exploited by land developers and speculators. The countryside was undergoing a phenomenal change, being transformed from a wilderness into an inland empire. Many of these settlers had been successful farmers in New England, Pennsylvania, New Jersey, and the Virginia Colony.

Geneva, Canandaigua and Bath had already become busy commercial centers. The U.S. Government had established a weekly mail route between Whitestown and Canandaigua as early as 1791. Letters were protected

1

from the weather in large morocco pocketbooks of post-riders such as Luther Cloe of Canandaigua or Jason Parker of Utica. When the letters were pulled from the coat breast-pocket, the clamor resembled a latter-day mail call at an Army camp.

Up to 1797, the Genesee Road was little more than a well-beaten swath through the forests then covering the country. Finally the New York State Legislature established a lottery, some of the proceeds of which were earmarked to improve this road.

The enthusiasm shown by the inhabitants for this new road was unparalleled. They volunteered their services to aid the State Commissioner of Roads by subscribing 4,000 days of work, which they performed in a cheerful, positive manner.

Through spring and into the summer of 1797 they toiled and labored on the road with picks and shovels. In the short space of 90 days, the road was transformed from an old Indian trail into a 64-foot wide, graveled highway.

The great improvement of this road afforded excellent opportunity for the stagecoach proprietors to extend their business westward. Innkeepers John House of Utica and Thomas Powell of Geneva jointly announced the establishment of a line of stages into the western country. Powell, an Englishman, was proprietor of the celebrated Geneva Hotel.

Stagecoach service between Utica and Geneva was inaugurated September 20, 1797. The first trip took three days, arriving in Geneva in the afternoon of the third day with four passengers.

With the newly-improved road came a wave of prosperity and settlement. In the space of four months after its completion, some 50 families had settled along the Genesee Road. Settlers continued to flow in a steady stream.

Soon, stages were operating weekly from Albany as far west as Canandaigua. Thus was laid the foundation for the enterprising "Old Line Mail." It was largely through the efforts of Jason Parker of Utica this grand

monopoly came into being. In 1794 he had established a
stage line between Utica and Albany in association with
several others. He fell heir to the Canandaigua line in
1802.

An early step towards a grand monopoly was a petition to the State Legislature, dated February 3, 1804,
The ancient document, found among the Assembly papers in the State Library in Albany, reads in part:

". . . that your petitioners conceive it necessary and
are desirous that a line of stages to run from the Village
of Utica in the County of Oneida to the town of Canandaigua in the County of Ontario shall be established. And
that in the present imperfect state of the turnpike road
leading from Utica to Canandaigua no individual can,
without manifest loss or injury to himself so long as rival
stages are permitted, continue a line of stages on the road
aforesaid for more than three months in each year. And
that the said aforesaid must of necessity continue in a
very imperfect state for several years to come.

"To remedy the evil and keep up a regular correspondence between the places aforesaid, as well for the benefit of Merchants and others trading in the Western district and for the citizens at large your petitioners humbly
pray that a law may be passed under such regulations
and restrictions as the legislature shall think meet and
proper, granting to said Jason Parker and Levi Stephens
the exclusive right of running stage from Utica to Canandaigua for the term of Ten years . . ." It is interesting
to note "Stephens" is the way his name is spelled in the
petition, but the actual signature is "Stevens."

Stevens and Parker got their "exclusive right" by a
State law passed March 31, 1804. The grant was for seven
years, not 10. The fine for infringing on this franchise was
$500. Among the stipulations in the act were:

— That the fare shall not exceed five cents a mile,
"with the liberty to every such passenger of taking with
him such carriage fourteen pounds weight of baggage,
and that for every one hundred and fifty pounds weight

The two major hotels in Upstate New York west of Albany before 1800 were Bagg's Tavern in Utica, erected about 1795, and the Geneva Hotel in Geneva, opened in 1796. Stagecoach service was inaugurated between these two places in 1797. *(Photo of Geneva Hotel courtesy of Geneva Historical Society.)*

of baggage over and above such fourteen pounds of weight as aforesaid, the sum of five cents for every mile shall be paid, and so in proportion for any greater or less quantity . . .'

— That such stage waggons or waggon or sleighs, shall proceed at least twice in every week, between June 1 and October 1. The route between Utica and Canandaigua was to be traversed within 48 hours — unavoidable accidents the exception.

— The stage was to be limited to seven adults with their usual baggage. More could be carried only by the unanimous consent of "the seven." Whenever a minimum of four more over the seven applied for passage, the proprietors were obliged to fit out an "extra."

— Any number less than four wanting transportation for more than 10 miles could book an "extra" by paying the fare of four passengers, and six cents a mile.

Stevens purchased two stagecoaches from John Nicholas of Geneva, who came to this area from Hampstead, Virginia, in the fall of 1803. Nicholas, prominent in Geneva history, fostered the famed White Springs Farm. The coaches were made on his plantation in Hampstead by slave labor.

Nicholas, his family, slaves and servants left Virginia on October 21, 1803. Each coach was pulled by four horses, with postillions riding the leaders. Other members of the family rode horseback or in a phaeton. The help made the journey in four-horse wagons, or on foot.

The following spring, Stevens started his new stage line. His advertisement, appearing in the May 15, 1804, issue of the *Western Repository* of Canandaigua, stated:

MAIL STAGE

The Public are respectfully informed, that the subscriber will run a Mail Stage from Canandaigua during the present season, once in each week. — He has been in great pains and expence to fit his Stages for the accommodations of Passenger.

Those persons who may wish to adopt this method of travelling to Utica, Albany, &c. may procure seats by applying at Taylor's Hotel, in Canandaigua, or at Powell's Hotel, in Geneva.

The Stage is only four days in running between the first mentioned places. The terms for each Passenger are five cents per mile.

LEVI STEVENS

Geneva, May 14.

The *Western Repository* of July 24, 1804, reported the same stage now would run twice a week, leaving Canandaigua every Sunday and Wednesday afternoon for the duration of the season. During winter months in the early years there was very little travel over the roads, which at times were impassable for weeks.

Although large expenditures had been made to put the Genesee Road in good condition, no provisions were made to keep it in repair. Maintenance was virtually non-existent. This was a common phenomenon all over the state.

So rapid had been emigration into this new land, particularly from New England, all ordinary resources were found inadequate to satisfy the demands for roads. Hence the system of establishing turnpike companies was resorted to.

Soon the spirit of turnpiking spread over every part of the state, starting just prior to 1800. Benjamin De Witt, commenting on the turnpike fever, observed in 1807:

"The prospect of increasing the value of lands by the establishment of good roads — the expectation of profit from the tolls granted by the legislature, and the more fascinating project of speculating in turnpike stock, induced a large part of the community to embark a part of their capitals for these purposes. The spirit of turnpiking consequently spread over every part of the country."

At De Witt's writing, there were 88 incorporated turnpike and bridge companies, representing $5½ million in capital, for a total of 20 large bridges and 3,000 miles of turnpike road; 900 miles of which was completed and in operation.

The Genesee Road from Utica to Canandaigua came under the jurisdiction of the Seneca Road Company, or "Seneca Turnpike," incorporated April 1, 1800, with a capital stock of $110,000. The road was to be six rods wide, and cleared that width of all timber, except ornamental trees. The road surface was to be 28 feet wide, made of the best materials, in a gradual arch not less than 20 inches higher than the outer edge. At least 18 feet of the bed was to be bedded with stone or wood to secure a solid foundation.

The theory was enough could be realized from turnpike tolls to maintain the road and return a dividend to the stockholders. Although contributing greatly to the internal growth of Upstate New York, turnpikes were generally poor investments. Usually maintenance costs fostered either shrunken dividends or none at all. After the Erie Canal was completed in 1825, toll receipts dropped off sharply, especially on the Seneca, and so-called "Cherry Valley" turnpikes.

Stockholders often regarded turnpikes as a means to an end; that they were satisfied for being indirectly benefited from the growth they stimulated. The returns of the Seneca Turnpike to the end of its existence in 1852 rarely exceeded four per cent.

For some years previous to its being abandoned as an unprofitable venture, the Seneca Turnpike was subjected to great complaint due to its condition. This resulted in a forfeiture of the charter and the road was turned over to the respective communities for maintenance.

Most of the turnpikes met with a similar fate. But certainly the stage proprietors benefited by having new and better roads to the far-flung districts of the state . . . even if there was a 25 cent levy on stagecoaches every 10 miles.

Chapter 2

Westward Expansion

Creation and ultimate completion of the Ontario & Genesee Turnpike afforded opportunuity to extend stage-coach service to Buffalo and Niagara Falls. Incorporated on April 2, 1805, the company was empowered to construct a toll road from Canandaigua to Black Rock, a distance of 90 miles.

John Metcalf applied for, and received an exclusive franchise from the State Legislature in April, 1807, to operate stagecoaches from Canandaigua to Buffalo. The "exclusive right" was good for seven years, and carried similar restrictions as in Stevens' franchise between Utica and Canandaigua.

Tuesday, May 10, 1808, the following appeared in the *Western Repository:*

WESTERN MAIL STAGE

The subscriber informs the public that he intends carrying the Mail from this town to Niagara in a STAGE COACH, to commence on the 1st Monday of May next, under the following regulations, viz:

Will leave Canandaigua every Monday at 6 O'Clock; A.M. and arrive at Niagara, by way of Buffaloe, every Thursday, at 9, A.M. Leave Niagara every Thursday at 3, P.M. and arrive at Buffaloe on Friday, at 5, P.M. Leave Buffaloe the same evening and arrive at Canandaigua the Sunday following at 5, P.M.

The subscriber informs the Ladies and Gentlemen that he has furnished himself with a convenient carriage and good horses, and that no attention on his part shall be wanting to render their seats pleasant and agreeable.

Rates of fare will be 6 cents per mile, including 14 Lbs. baggage.

JOHN METCALF

Canandaigua, April 26, 1808

The stagecoach business continued to progress and thrive. On July 5, 1813, William Powell, proprietor of the Geneva Hotel, commenced running a *daily* line between Canandaigua and Utica. The stage left Canandaigua at 4 A.M., except Sunday, arriving in Utica at 4 P.M. the following day. By this arrangement, travelers could go to Albany and return in three days.

The stagecoach drew up to Taylor's Hotel in Canandaigua, received its passengers, and then started off with the crack of whip and rumble of wheels down the street. Said an observer, "the rate diminished with increase of distance till a steady gate was taken, and then for hours, looking upon the growing villages, the passing travel, conversing with pleasant companions, or settling to a nap, unconscious of jar or jolt, time or distance."

The establishment of these stage lines indicates the advancing routes of travel. A long period of slow but steady development followed. After the War of 1812 there was a noticeable quickening of staging activity. A new line of tri-weekly stages commenced running between Albany and Onondaga Hollow, via Cherry Valley, on November 2, 1813. The night lay-over was at Cherry Valley which had a number of taverns.

Farther west, tri-weekly service from Canandaigua to Buffalo came in 1814, and to Rochester in 1817. Between 1814 and 1820, stage lines radiated in all directions from Canandaigua.

The "Old Line" pretty well controlled the major stage routes after 1816, although there were occasional com-

Stage service from Canandaigua to Rochester commenced in 1817, via Victory, Fisher's and Pittsford.

petitors. Competition was usually short-lived since the "Old Line" had most of the mail contracts, and the confidence of discriminating travelers.

In 1816 Oliver Phelps of Ludlowville established a line between Newburgh and Canandaigua, and Ithaca and Auburn. He and Conradt Teeter, a well-known stage driver in the Southern Tier, and in northern Pennsylvania, were granted an exclusive franchise over these routes on February 14, 1816.

Phelps, one of the most enterprising men of his day, was largely responsible for the first steamboat on Cayuga Lake, the "Enterprise," which made her maiden voyage on June 1, 1820. The boat connected with his line of stages.

Later his name was associated with construction work on the Erie and Welland Canals. He moved to St. Catharines, Ontario. Canada, in 1824 and was one of the leading businessmen and citizens of that city until his death in 1851.

Segments of the route across New York State were divided among the various "Old Line" proprietors. Parker's teams brought the stage to Manlius, where the Sherwood teams were hitched on to make the run to Canandaigua. Teams operated in the "rounds," that is, "first in, first out."

For instance, Norman Maxon of Elbridge might be in Fayetteville. "My team had been in the stable longest, and I would hitch on and draw it to Syracuse, where another team would take it and go on to Camillus. When it came my turn I would follow to Camillus and then in order to Elbridge and lastly to Auburn, where I would turn. On the down trip stops were made at the same changing places until I got to Fayetteville."

The same method of relays prevailed all along the "Old Line" system to Buffalo. The advantage of such a course was it gave horses shorter runs and eliminated delays caused by the feeding and watering of horses.

Another feature of stagecoach travel was the "waybill," which every driver carried. For instance, if a person in Buffalo wanted to go to Albany he would go to the stage office, register his name and destination with the agent and pay the fare. Thus, with the exception of "way" passengers, the driver was relieved of the burden of collecting fares and making change.

Maxon said, "we carried the mail, too, and the distribution was done at each Post Office along the route except the through mails. Very few newspapers were carried, as people had not got to reading them. I think we would bring about five into Elbridge, one of them going to the hotel and the other four supplying the town with its weekly reading matter."

Another Sherwood driver, Adolphus Newton, at one time drove the "Telegraph" or express coach. This was

Canandaigua, Auburn, Utica, Cherry-Valley and Albany
STAGES.

LEAVE Canandaigua every *Monday, Wednesday* and *Friday*, at 3 o'clock, A. M. and arrive at Utica, *Tuesday, Thursday* and *Saturday* at 8 A. M. and at Albany, at 7 P. M.

Leave Utica on Tuesday, Thursday and Saturday, at 3 A. M. and arrive at Albany same day.

Leave Albany, on *Monday, Wednesday* and *Friday*, at 4 o'Clock, A. M.; and Utica, at 3 P. M. and arrive at Canandaigua, on *Tuesday, Thursday* and *Saturday*.

Also, a STAGE, which leaves Auburn, every *Monday, Wednesday* and *Friday*, at 6 A. M. and arrives at Ithica, the same day. Leaves Ithica, on Tuesday, Thursday and Saturday, at 6 A. M. and arrives at Auburn the same day.

ALL Baggage at the risk of the owner. Seats taken at the Eagle Tavern, and Loomis's Northern, Western and Eastern Stage House, No. 494, South-Market-street, Albany; York House, Utica; E. C. Kingsley's, Canandaigua; C. Coe's, Auburn; A. Camp's, Skeneatles; and at Mr. Morse's Inn, Manlius.

H. D. BEMAN, Canandaigua,
O. PHELPS & Co. Ludlow-Ville,
R. P. CANDE, Auburn,
E. MONTGOMERY, Sangersfield,
J. B. SWAN, Albany,
J. BRANCH, Ditto, Proprietors.

who assure the public, that their horses are the best kind—their drivers experienced and careful, and that every possible attention will be paid to render the Traveller's situation agreeable, while travelling in those Lines.

N. B. From Canandaigua to Buffaloe, the Stage runs six times a week; and from Canandaigua to Lewiston, via Rochester, three times a week—going through in two days.

Auburn, October 8, 1816.

ALBANY and AUBURN
STAGES.

The subscribers in addition to their Stages, which leave CANANDAIGUA and UTICA, six times in each week, and run through in one day and an half, are now running a Stage, which leaves CANANDAIGUA and ALBANY every MONDAY, WEDNESDAY and FRIDAY, at 2 o'clock, A. M. going by the way of AUBURN, SKANEATELES, ONONDAGA, MANLIUS, CAZENOVIA, MADISON and CHERRY VALLEY, in two days.

ALSO,
A Stage, which runs from AUBURN,

Every MONDAY, WEDNESDAY and FRIDAY, at 5 o'clock, A. M. passing through BRUTUS, CAMILLUS, GEDDESBURGH and SALINA, to MANLIUS, at which place it arrives in season for their CHERRY VALLEY and UTICA Stages; returning from MANLIUS by the same rout, leaves MANLIUS every TUESDAY, THURSDAY and SATURDAY, and arrives at AUBURN the same day, where the UTICA and CANANDAIGUA Stages arrive the succeeding day, at sun rise,

Thomas Powell,
Jason Parker, & Co.
Israkiah Wetmore,
Leonard Baker,
Jesse Campbell,
Aaron Thorp, Jun.
Isaac Sherwood, & Co.

Dated September 13, 1816.

N. B. Seats taken in Auburn at Mr. Coe's Tavern.

Ancient newspaper ads reveal stiff competition between two lines of stages on the "Cherry Valley" route between Albany and Canandaigua, as well as through the Mohawk Valley.

RULES AND REGULATIONS,

FOR THE GATE KEEPERS

OF THE

Third Great Western Turnpike Road Company.

1. It is expected and required that every gate keeper will give his personal attention to the business of his office; and not leave the gate to the care of his family, or any other person, more than is unavoidably necessary.—Farming and gate tending are incompatible.

2. The gate to be kept down or shut at all times, day and night, except when raised or opened for the object, for which it was erected. At night, when the gate keeper goes to bed, the gate must be shut down and locked; and if necessary for the accommodation of travellers, the gate keeper must get up. A violation of these rules would be a breach of the gate keeper's bond.

3. The gate keeper is not obliged by law to raise or open the gate until the toll is paid, if the person wishing to pass is not exempt by law from paying toll.

4. No person to pass the gate free of toll, except those specified in the act of incorporation—which is as follows:

"Any person passing to or from public worship, "his farm, a funeral, or to or from any mill or mills, "or to or from any blacksmith-shop within three "miles, to which he usually resorts, or for a physi- "cian," to pass the gate free of toll.

5. No credit to be given for toll, or to commuters.

6. The toll money received during the day at the gate, to be set down upon the book every night; also the names of commuters and the amount of money received from them, separate and by itself, and the money put in some secure place. A small sum in change, not exceeding one dollar, may be reserved out of the amount set down upon the book, for change the next day. The amount set down at night upon the book may be in even dollars or quarters; and the book will show at the end of the month, and at the end of the year, the sum received every day for toll, except the change reserved the first day. It may vary a few cents when more change is reserved one day than is first reserved. But there can be no great variation, if not more than a dollar is at first reserved, and not exceeded. No relaxation of this rule will be tolerated in the gate keepers.

7. At the end of the month, the money ought exactly to agree with the total amount on the book, exclusive of the change reserved. If they do not agree, the gate keeper must state it to the treasurer, (if there is any great variation) or make up the deficiency himself. If the money on hand is more than the amount on book, it is evident there has been a mistake in entering it on the book. If the money and book do not agree, and there should be any great deficiency, the presumption is strong that the difference arises from some other cause than mistake in entering it on book; for the money then is counted in small parcels. The *book* must not be *altered* to agree with the *money*, but the excess or deficiency must be stated at the foot of the monthly returns.

8. No toll money must be used, borrowed or lent by the gate keeper, on any pretence whatever; and the money must be kept securely, where it is not accessible to children, and others not concerned in tending the gate.

9. On the first day of every month the gate keepers must make their monthly returns of all the money received at the gate, in the following form:

First, the daily receipts of the toll, agreeable to the printed form, and the amount added up.

Second, the Stage toll must be put on the returns by itself, and under the footing of the daily receipts.

Third, the names of persons commuting must be put on the monthly returns, and the price for which each commutes, separate from the daily receipts of the toll and stage money; and the amount added to the stage and daily receipts; making an aggregate of all the money received during the month.

10. After returns have been completed as above required, they must be sent by mail, sealed, and directed to the Treasurer.

11. RULES FOR COMMUTING.

First.—All persons commuting, and travelling five miles on the road, to pay *half* the sum of what in the estimation of the gate keeper and commute director, would be the probable legal toll for a year.

Second.—Persons travelling three miles upon the road, to pay *one third* of the amount, of what would be the legal toll for a year, in the estimation of the gate keeper and commute director.

Third.—No person can commute, who travels over five miles upon the road.

The above Rules are to govern the gate keepers, but may in some cases be varied at the discretion of the commute director.

Fourth.—No person to commute for less than 50 cents.

Fifth.—No person can commute at two gates.

Sixth.—All commutations to expire on the first Monday in February.

Tollgate house operated as a toll bridge by Cayuga & Seneca Road Bridge Co. — 1843 — Circa 1890. (Location of old free bridge and Menard bridge on Route 5 and 20)

a stage with a limited number of passengers, carrying the mail. When roads were good, it averaged eight miles per hour. Newton said horses were changed every 10 miles, but one driver went through from Auburn to Manlius, 33 miles. He said on important occasions, when he carried notables, he made the distance in three hours.

Once, Newton carried Governor William H. Seward. On another occasion he had Chief Black Hawk and eight lesser chieftans of the Sac Tribe aboard. The coach covered 10 miles in 50 minutes. The "Telegraph" run utilized the newest coaches and finest teams. Chief Black Hawk for a few moments forgot his role as a federal prisoner and became an enthusiastic and admiring witness to Newton's skill with the reins.

But Black Hawk's love for stagecoach adventures

took a turn for the worse when a not-so-skilled driver in Pennsylvania lost control of the team. The Indian chief and his companions, after a wild dash down-hill, ended up in a deep pool of mud.

During their careers, Newton and Maxon claimed such notable passengers as General Winfield Scott, Martin Van Buren, and state and federal figures of varied importance. It was the rule to fit out "extras" or special runs for these people.

Famous personalities left impressions with Maxon. He said, "while I was in Syracuse William L. Marcy (one-time Governor of New York) would come to our office and hire a team and driver to take him to General Mann's. I took him the first time he went. He would always ask for me after that. I had a fine gray team and it became a favorite of his.

"General Scott went up the line with me once. He was on his way to Fort Erie, and wore a military cloak and cap. When he got out at Elbridge he made me think of a pair of tongs, he was so tall and thin, but afterward he fleshed up."

Newton had little use for Enos T. Throop of Auburn, also a governor of New York State. "He was a very selfish person and had no regard for the comforts of others. One morning I was called up to take him to Weedsport to catch the packet. It was late in the fall and the day was cold and stormy.

"It was the last packet east that season and he was anxious to get it." Throop's home, "Willowbrook," was near the foot of Owasco Lake. The night before departing to Weedsport, Throop went to the stage office and ordered a turn-out. That night, he stayed in the village of Auburn with his brother, George.

"I was at the house at the time agreed upon," Maxon said, "but Throop was not ready. He sent out word that he was eating his breakfast. It was a full hour before he got outside. We began quarrelling before we got outside the village, and kept it up until we reached Weedsport. We got there just as the packet drew up to the dock."

A frequent stage passenger was Francis Granger of Canandaigua, one-time U.S. Postmaster, politician and promoter, who "was a constant traveller and was very popular with the boys." One year, he ran for governor on the anti-Masonic ticket, but lost the election. The following spring, Maxon said, he was riding in the coach with Granger, Jess Williams driving the stage.

"It was a raw day and Frank got chilled before reaching Syracuse. When we got out of the stage he lectured Jess about the poor run from Camillus. Williams replied: 'Say, mass Granger, I guess I'se made as good a run as you did last fall when you run for anti-Mason Guvnor.' Granger was so pleased with the retort that he gave Williams a new buffalo robe which he had with him."

United States Bank President Nicholas Biddle once was returning east from Niagara Falls, and was in a great hurry. "Colonel Sherwood called on me to take him from Auburn to Elbridge," Maxon said. "His instructions were to make the trip in forty minutes, the usual time being an hour and fifteen minutes. I did it and it was considered a very creditable feat. It would not be thought much of a drive now with a light wagon, but you must recollect our stages weighed 2,400 pounds."

Chapter 3

Knights of the Road

"Although nobody, I believe, ever travelled a hundred miles by land in this country, without being overturned, the drivers deserve infinite credit for the rare occurrence of accidents. How they can carry a coach at all over some of their roads is miraculous; and high praise is due to them, both for care and skill, that any body, in any part of this country, ever arrives at the end of a land journey." So wrote Frances Anne Butler in her journal of 1835.

The old-time stage drivers were a daring lot, but generally faithful to the performance of their duties. To their good judgment, skill and energy, multitudes owed the safety of life and limb. Considering the number of stages that plied the roads through the years, contemporary accounts of accidents are few in number.

Hirman Reed of Marcellus related an instance demonstrating the skill of a driver. While attending school in Skaneateles, he and a fellow school-mate, wishing to go to Auburn by stage, climbed up on the box with the driver. While descending the steepest hill between the two towns one of the pole straps leading from the front of the pole to the collars of the wheel horses broke. These were the straps used to hold back the stage.

Ready for the emergency the driver cracked his whip and the horses dashed down the hill at a full gallop. He did this to maintain a constant draft on the pole to which the leader horses were hooked. The coach halted at the bottom of the hill, passengers and horses unharmed. It was Reed's last ride on the "box."

17

Stage drivers were generally considerate of their passengers and their safety, although occasional accidents were inevitable. Many paintings, such as this by the famed E. L. Henry, depict riders on the "box" with the driver. However, this practice was generally frowned upon for safety's sake. *(New York State History Collection, Office of State History)*

Hiram K. Stimson, a stage-driver-turned-preacher, commented on this class of people in his 1874 volume, *From the Stage Coach to the Pulpit*. He endeavored to correct a false impression that drivers were an unfeeling, worthless class of beings. He admitted many were exceeding profane and intemperate. But despite their rough and uncouth exteriors they were generous and frank.

"I have known one to pull off his overcoat in a cold winter's day and give it to a sick passenger inside, while, at the same time, a 'broadcloth gentleman' of the legal profession would not even give the sick man the hind seat of the couch, thus compelling him to ride on the middle seat, rather than give up an iota of his comfort."

Stimson wrote: "And having been one of the craft in the childhood of the stage coach in this country, I want to record my testimony to the noble-heartedness of the professional stage driver." He said the driver had feelings for all classes, especially his comrades and needy people. He could drive from one point to another, "with no human habitation to mark the road, the darkest night that ever was, with all the certainty of instinct."

Drivers were a sporting and competitive lot. With so many lines in business, racing was the natural consequence. Eventually the State Legislature mandated laws imposing severe penalties for this sport. The first law was enacted on April 11, 1817, entitled, "An Act relative to the running of stages." A fine of $100 per month would be imposed on the proprietor as long as a driver in his employ was "addicted to drunkeness."

A driver would be fined $5.00 for running his team, or preventing another stage to pass him. The same act also stipulated a ceiling of seven cents a mile as the maximum passengers could be charged. Local courts were empowered to prosecute offenders.

The public and the press were quick to admonish the actions of drivers. The *Lyons Advertiser* editor wrote on June 18, 1823: "Under a late act of parliament, the driver of a stage coach has been convicted of manslaughter in having furiously driven his coach, upset and killed a passenger. The Judge, in passing sentence, said he could transport him for life; but as this was the first offence under the new law, he gave him a suitable admonition and ordered him to be imprisoned twelve months at hard labour on the stepping mill.

"An application of this law to some of our own cases would have a most salutary effect. There is in fact no means of punishing a coachman who drives furiously and jeapordizes the lives of his passengers. Very frequently

Mry Ives
K
Stillman Kelly
Capt Giles Kellogg

Martha Waldron
Elizabeth Waldron
Nancy Wier

SOL. *VAN RENSSELAER, P. M.*

TO THE PUBLIC.
POST COACH:
T. Powell, & Co.

HAVE this day removed their *Mail Coach Office*, in Albany, from No. 2. Green Street, to

No. 365 *North Market-Street*,

Near the two Mansion Houses and Post Office, and continue to run their coaches, as usual, from Albany to Buffalo, via Schenectady, Utica, Auburn, and Canandaigua:—Also, from Albany via Cherry Valley, Manlius, Auburn, Canandaigua, and Rochester to Lewiston :—Likewise, from Cherry Valley to Cooperstown.

The Diligence Coach will continue to leave Albany for Schenectady every afternoon, for the accommodation of those who wish to sleep at Schenectady.

Extras, with regular changes of horses through the lines, will at all times be furnished, on short notice, and at reasonable prices.

The obligation which the subscribers feel themselves under to the public, for their many past favours, and their duty as mail contractors, prompts them to exertions, which will leave nothing undone for the comfort and expeditious travelling of their customers.

All BAGGAGE at the risk of the owner,

T. POWELL & Co.

N. B.—Passengers will be taken up and set down at any place in Albany, where they may direct.
January 1st, 1823.   33tf

MACHINE CARDS,

ORDERS received for cotton and wool machine cards, and furnished by one of the most approved makers at the shortest notice, by
GODFREY & TOWNSEND.
Albany, Dec. 18, 1822.   34m2

Old time newspaper ads espoused excellent drivers and accommodations, although in reality they often left much to be desired. This ad was in the *Albany Argus*, January 7, 1823.

they turn a deaf ear to the entreaty of a passenger to drive with moderation. The customs of taking a drink at stopping places and racing with rival coaches has been productive of fatal consequences. A few wholesome examples would introduce a new state of things!"

An amendment to the 1817 law, passed November 24, 1824, made the proprietors liable for certain acts of their drivers and responsible to the parties injured through negligence. Again, it was left to the local courts for prosecution. The fine was now not to exceed $100, or six months' imprisonment.

Further legislation was enacted April 17, 1826, entitled "An Act for the safety of Passengers in Steam-Boats, and of Travellers by Land and by Water." This law is a masterpiece of legal jargon. Drivers would now be fined $20 for preventing another coach to pass. Racing was punishable by a fine not exceeding $50, or 60 days in jail. It was illegal to leave horses unattended; hitched to the coach while passengers were aboard, "without first making fast with a sufficient halter, rope or chain, or by placing the lines in the hands of some other person, so as to prevent their running."

Drivers also would be liable for any damages resulting from negligence. The laws, like so many others on the books, went unenforced to a great degree, as fierce competition ensued as long as stages operated. The few accounts recorded of accidents are usually sympathetic towards the driver, who was often a victim of circumstances beyond his control.

In 1822 an elderly traveler was killed near Cherry Valley after he was knocked down by horses drawing a stage with 11 passengers aboard. The driver was not blamed as he was unable to stop in time. Apparently the old man was deaf and did not react to repeated shouts from the driver. On another occasion a wagon ran against the lead horses of a stage just east of Geneva. The coach was forced off the road, and the pole or "tongue" was sheered off, as well as one of the forewheels. The driver, perfectly cool, held the reins while the passengers scrambled to safety.

The only casualty was a man who broke his nose and sprained his ankle after he jumped from his seat next to the driver. The passengers extricated themselves from the "stage wreck" and congratulated each other on their fortunate escape. This caused an hour's delay while they sent back to Geneva for another coach.

The stage driver was a natural lover of horses. As a result he became skilled in the management of his teams, teaching the horses many tricks. Each horse had a name, and when called upon, obeyed the mandates of his master. The driver's whip consisted of a stalk from four to six feet long. At one end was a neatly-braided silk cracker.

With great dexterity the drivers handled the reins of four-horse teams and wielded the whip, giving it a smart

Rain or shine, stagecoach travel went on for decades, and drivers weren't always fortunate enough to have umbrellas as depicted in this E. L. Henry painting.

crack over the leaders' ears. To all it was an enchanting sight to watch the stage come down the hill at full speed — the driver holding the reins in one hand and cracking his whip with the other. Entering a town or nearing the tavern, he'd lay the whip down and blow his horn to signal his arrival.

He tightens the reins of whirls off with a fling
From the roof of the coach his ten feet of string;
Now lightly he flicks the 'nigh' leader's left ear,

Gives the wheelers a neighborly slap with the stock,
They lay back their ears as the coach gives a rock
And strike a square trot in the tick of a clock!

There's a jumble, a jar and a gravelly trill
In the craunch of the wheels on the slate-stone hill
That grind up the miles like a grist in a mill.

He touches the bay and he talks to the brown,
Sends a token of silk, a word and a frown.
To the filly whose heels are too light to stay down.

Chapter 4

The "Tavern Era"

"The prices of travelling in stages, and of living in some hotels are too high, when compared with the general fall of commodities and wages. It is true that the horn of plenty scatters its blessings in profusion.

"Your breakfast and tea table is overloaded with cakes, green cucumbers, pickled cucumbers, cheese, sweetmeats and sallad, besides more agreeable viands, but then the coffee is sometimes burnt (not roasted) so that the aroma escapes; or you have a deleterious green tea instead of black — and instead of wholesome bread, you are served a mixture of flour and milk, which is really disgusting; because as soon as the latter ingredient acidifies, it taints the whole mass, and offends the smell as well as the taste.

"The bacon and eggs, at dinner, and the broiled chicken and veal cutlets are very fine. You have good beer and cider — fine wine is rarely to be got and in this country of cheap timber, the use of ice houses are comparatively rare.

"When you call for a meal, you are frequently surprised to find yourself surrounded by strange travellers. This is a contrivance of Madame Trateur to have trouble —and then it is considered an essential etiquette to place a neatly dressed female at table, to preside over its ceremonies, and to pour out the coffee. This is frequently very agreeable and you are often pleased with the conversation of a modest, sensible young woman."

This is a typical reaction of a stagecoach traveler on

his way across New York State following his stay at a
tavern in June, 1820.

Taverns came in natural sequence after roads opened
the country for settlement. And as crude as some of them
might have been, they played an important role in the
life of the pioneer settlements.

Local histories refer to many important events trans-
piring under the roof of the local tavern, which in earliest
times was the center of local activities of more or less
local importance. To its doors the post rider and later the
stage driver brought the mail. It served as the place of
entertainment, as well as restaurant and hotel.

Hundreds of taverns, inns, hotels and coffee-houses
(depending on what the proprietor wished to call it)
lined the major and lateral roads and turnpikes. They
flanked all principal roads leading into town. They were
supported primarily by transient travel in times of immi-
gration and settlement.

Emigrants on foot, horseback and in wagons poured
in a continual stream from east to west to the then-
wilderness of western New York and Ohio. Stagecoaches
loaded inside and out with travelers tore through the
countryside at the rate of three or four miles an hour.

The driver's tin horn sounded over hill and dale to
alert the landlord of the coach's impending approach —
that meals might be in readiness for famished passengers.
Stablemen made ready the change of horses. Soon, the
steaming teams, followed by the coach, appeared on the
crest of the hill or at the curve in the road.

The horses soon gained sight of their accustomed
stopping place, where they knew they would find rest and
nourishment. This gave the animals renewed vigor.
Pricking up their ears, they pulled up to the door in great
pomp and flourish; the old coach creaking and straining
at every joint.

Hurriedly, the passengers disembarked, hastening into
the tavern to satisfy their appetites and tragedy life while
the horses were changed. A bewildered Englishman once
exclaimed, "The stream rushes in and dribbles out as at

List of Inns from Utica to Canandaigua:

Thomas	Miles	2
Russels		3
Congers Newhartford		4
Cousins		
Davis		6
Greens		
Clarks		8
Cooks		
Pixleys		9
Hecox		
Larrds Westmoreland		11
Leavens		12
Marshalls Vernon		14
Gays		17
Williams		20
Persons		
Otis Oneida Castle		22
Young		23
Sherwins Lenox		24
Olcots		25
Wimples		26
Smalleys		29
Benedicts		29
Blakesley Sullivan		31
Douglas		31
Clocks		32
Clark		33
Pearsons		33
Wilsons		34
Warner Manlius		38
Dyer		39
Dwight		40
Barrit		
Gumver		43
Olmsted		45
Cadwell East Hill		47
Brown		48

Longstreet Onda. Hallow	50
Johnsons West Hill	52
Brownsons	
Hutchinson Marsellus	55
Leonard	55
Lawrence	58
Beach 9 Mile Creek	60
Gumver	63
Hall Skeneatcles	66
Sherwood	
Hatch Brutes	67
Amermam Auborn	73
Tracy	
Bostwich	
Ponroy	
Huggins Aurelius	75
Cross	76
Goodwin	77
Comsrock	78
G. Hall	80
Buckley Cayuga	82
Harris	
Morris	
Chapman Redmills	83
Miller	
Birdsall	86
Smith	
Sampson	92
Dobins	93
Shield Geneva	96
Powels	
Taylor Seneca	101
Ball	103
Whitney Gorham	107
Doty Canandaigua	112
Lamberton	
Bates	113

From Canandaigua to Buffaloe.

Steel or Beach	6
Saxions	10
Egleston West Bloomfield	11
Mills	13
Frost Lima	16
Persons	20
Hosmers	24
Smith	28
Camerous Caledonia	31
Davis	35
Ganson	37
Mrs. Berry	38
Lemon	43
Churchel	45

Phelps	47
Loomis Batavia	49
Thomas	52
Bruce	56
Richardson	60
Lesters	63
Parmele	65
Spurr	70
Porter	75
Harris	76
Sharps	80
Atkins	85
Miller	87
Ransome Buffaloe	90

Lists of the major taverns on the road from Utica to Buffalo were published regularly in William Williams' Almanac of Utica from the earliest days of staging through the 1820s.

Typical of the scores of country taverns on the great western route was Ramsey's (later Westover's) at Half Acre. west of Auburn. There were three taverns at this four corners, that, at one time, had an unenviable reputation for morality.

breakfast and the room is clear in less than a quarter of an hour!"

Momentarily, the driver cries out "all aboard" and the passengers clamor to regain their seats in the coach. The driver cracks his whip and they are off. Rolling through the afternoon, they pass tavern after tavern, averaging a mile apart on many stretches of road — many with swinging picture sign. Finally, they stop for supper, a taproom evening and the night, uncertain of a private room; fortunate in some places to get a private bed.

Taverns also catered to drovers and teamsters, two classes who were often at odds with each other in contesting the road. Teamsters preferred the hard, well-crowned and drained road which made hauling easy. But such roads lame the cattle and the drovers preferred the springtime with its mud. Some tavern-keepers catered

Another of the "better classed" stopping places on the "Cherry Valley Turn-pike" was, and remains to this day, the Lincklaen House in Cazenovia. Built in 1835, it was named for John Lincklaen, land agent for the Holland Land Company, and founder of the village.

specifically to the wants of both, and so advertised their establishments as drover's inns.

These taverns thrived as long as loads of merchandise were freighted between Albany and Buffalo and intermediate points, and livestock were driven and coaxed to market. Man and beast must be fed and sheltered, and the tavern rose to the emergency.

A proprietor's income was not excessive. A shilling for a meal, six pence for lodging, 18 pence for stabling and feeding a team, three cents for "three fingers" of whiskey or six pence for a draught of brandy was a slow way of accumulating a fortune. But millionaires were rare in those days.

The typical country tavern was a farmhouse; a long two-story frame building set flush to the road. A "stoop" or platform extended the entire length of the building for the convenience of getting in and out of the coach. A door, midway of the front, opened into a hall, extending through the main portion of the house to the dining room (long room) in the rear.

To the left, as you entered, a door might lead to a plainly-furnished ladies' sitting room. Just beyond this door the stairs led to the rooms and, in some cases, a ball-room upstairs. Opposite the sitting room a door from the hall leads to the bar-room. Another entrance to this popular resort might be an outside door.

On one side of this room a large open fireplace afforded ample room for big blazing logs in winter. The bar in one corner exhibited decanters labeled "Whiskey," "Brandy," "Gin" or "Rum," in gilt lettering. To add to the effect, between the liquor decanters ranged glass cans of striped peppermint, or red-tinted wintergreen candles, and lemons. The assortment was completed by a few clay pipes, dull blue paper packages of fine-cut smoking tobacco, and perhaps one or two boxes of cigars on the top shelf.

Adjacent to the tavern stood the commodious barns and sheds, under which anyone might shelter his animals and feed without cost, if he brought his own fodder. Prominently in front of the tavern was the well, with its wooden pump and pail for watering the horses of any who chose to avail themselves of the privilege.

Also in front was the sign post, standing 12 feet high, surmounted by an oblong or elliptical sign board, decorated with trimmings. Here appeared the name of the proprietor — sometimes in black letters on a white background, sometimes in gilt letters on a dark blue background.

A traveler through Central New York in 1820 remarked: "The principal signs of taverns are descriptive of the genius and feelings of a people. In this country, the bald eagle, the symbol of national glory — the implements and products of agriculture, the signs of national wealth — and Masonic figures, the emblems of national charity, adorn the inns. Sometimes you meet with a

The Western Exchange Hotel in Auburn was classed as one of the finest hostelries along the route of the "Old Line Mail" in the 1820s. Lafayette was entertained here in 1825. *(Roger Coomber, photographer)*

Another famous establishment in western New York is the Frontier House in Lewiston, near Niagara Falls, in operation since the 1820s.

whale, a lion, or a horse — but where do you not see un-meaning and absurd exhibitions."

Tavern keepers, primarily in villages and cities, pub-licized their establishments prominently in newspapers of the day: "No noisy rabbles will be allowed a place in my house whereby the rest of the weary may be disturbed. Liquors and other refreshments of first quality will be furnished."

More or less everyone who lived in the community frequented the local tavern. In the winter, the oracle of the village occupied the best seat in front of the fire, and others ranged around in the order of importance. In the evening, the local magnates would drop into the bar-room, to gossip with the stage passengers.

Discussed were politics, crop prospects, and other local and national matters. A game of checkers was usu-ally in progress in some part of the room. When the spirit moved, one would approach the bar and take his bitters, drawing from the depths of his pocket the required three coppers.

At night, a traveler who objected to a stranger as a bedfellow was regarded as unreasonably fastidious. It was not uncommon, after a weary traveler had retired for the night, than to be awakened by the landlord, who appeared with a tallow candle, showing a stranger into his bed.

Although most taverns accommodated those seeking alcoholic refreshment, they had not yet assumed the un-auspicious connotation applied to them in later decades. But alcoholism was prevalent and there were massive temperance movements.

On August 11, 1810, DeWitt Clinton recorded in his journal: "Fourten miles from Ithaca, in the town of Spencer, Tioga County, is a settlement of Virginians called Speed; they are all Federalists. An old man by the name of Hyde belonging to it, spent at least five hours in the tavern to-day, and went off so drunk that he could hardly balance himself on his horse. Behind him was a bag, containing on each side a keg of liquor, and his

---

COUNTY OF SENECA, SS.

Be it remembered, That on the *fifth* day of *May* — — in the year of our *Lord* one thousand eight hundred and *twenty-nine Nelson Roosevelt Eyre* in the county aforesaid, Inn=Keeper, personally came before me *Thos. C, Magee* Esq. Justice of the peace for the said county, and acknowledged himself to owe to the People of the State of New=York, the sum of one hundred and twenty-five dollars, to be made and levied of his goods and chattels, lands and tenements, to the use of the said People if default shall be made in the condition underwritten.

WHEREAS the above bounden *Nelson Roosevelt* is Licensed to keep an Inn or Tavern from the *fifth* day of *May* instant, until the first Tuesday of May next, in the house where he now dwells, at *Eyre* aforesaid :

Now the Condition of this Recognizance is such, That if the said *Nelson Roosevelt* shall not, during the time he shall Keep an Inn or Tavern, Keep a disorderly Inn or Tavern, or suffer or permit any cock-fighting, gaming or playing with cards or dice, or keep any billiard table or other gaming table, or shuffle board within the Inn or Tavern by him to be kept, or within any out-house, yard or garden, belonging thereunto ; then this Recognizance shall be void, or otherwise remain in full force and effect.

Taken and acknowledged the day and year above written, before me,   *Nelson Roosevelt*

Thos, Magee Justice

In olden times, tavern keepers were licensed in many communities
throughout New York State. *(Arnold Barben collection)*

pockets were loaded with bottles. In the bar-room he abused Jefferson, Madison, and a number of other leading Republicans."

The country inns generally provided poor accommodations. There were always complaints of poor food, dirty linen, bed bugs, or snoring bed-partners.

The larger communities along the Buffalo Stage Route, such as Albany, Utica, and Geneva, boasted some of the finest hotels in the state prior to 1800. Albany had its celebrated Tontine Coffee-House; Utica with Bagg's Hotel, and Geneva, with its Geneva Hotel. All were operated by experienced proprietors who would not tolerate the unkempt conditions that were a way of life in country taverns.

The Tontine Coffee House on State Street in Albany was opened in 1798, and first operated by Ananias Platt, one of the pioneer stage operators in the vicinity. In May, 1801, it was taken over by Matthew Gregory. It was a house distinguished from all other public houses of that day, by the quiet order that reigned through all its departments; by its perfect neatness, and the total absence of a bar.

The higher rates of fare charged at the Tontine, and the fact that no liquors were sold except to its own boarders, nor ever seen except at the table, excluded the "low and thirsty." But it was always well filled. All travelers of any note or consequence; all foreigners of distinction; in a word, all gentlemen, put up at the Tontine.

For a period of 10 or 12 years, Mr. Gregory had no competition, no rival house to contend with; and was therefore compelled to make a fortune.

Gem of the "western country" was the Geneva Hotel, erected in 1796 by Charles Williamson, land agent for the famed Phelps and Gorham Purchase holdings. The basic structure still stands at the south corner of Washington Street and Park Place in Geneva.

Thomas Powell, an Englishman, was the first proprietor, and an old acquaintance of Williamson's from London, England. Powell emigrated to this country and

Cady Tavern in Moravia, so typical of its day, was the center of community life. It was a "general rendezvous" not only for stage travelers, but for political meetings and the like.

for a time operated a public house at Lansingburgh, near Albany.

At an early age, Powell became a stage proprietor, and was instrumental in establishing such service from Utica to Geneva in September, 1797. After keeping the hotel for several years, he moved to Schenectady in 1810 to look after the stage business, and was succeeded by his brother, William. DeWitt Clinton commented:

"Powell's Hotel was built by Capt. Charles Williamson, the agent of the Pulteney estate, who also laid out the south part of this village. It is a very large and expensive wooden building, and has, besides an ice-house and other appendages of a great establishment, a descending hanging-garden on the side of the lake. The fruit-trees, particularly the peach, apricot, and plumb, look remarkably vigorous and healthy."

As the municipalities grew more sophisticated, more elegant hotels sprang up, replacing the rural tavern in Syracuse, Auburn, Canandaiagua, Batavia and Rochester. But be it remembered that the country taverns were here first.

Visitors, travelers and settlers made such places necessary. The so-called proprietors of country inns were there to profit from an original necessity. For them, keeping tavern was synonymous with tilling the soil, land speculation and other pursuits.

A tavern of those days draws a similar parallel with the tourist home of the present century. Occasionally, the New York State Legislature endeavored to improve conditions at taverns by enacting laws. Although they set guidelines, they went generally unenforced.

Local governments licensed taverns on a yearly basis in many communities. But with the decline of patronage resulting from new modes of transportation, these laws fell into obsolescence.

Proprietors wishing to continue resorted to various devices to maintain an income. Dancing parties became more frequent, and at these and other gatherings immoderate drinking was encouraged, especially at taverns of waning fortunes. Public dances were quite the rage, and the ranking citizens of the community avidly participated. The whole neighborhood turned out for the festivities. The more dignified "inns" built in the towns in the 1820s and 1830s were able to adjust to the times by accommodating railroad travelers, while the country tavern host became an extinct species.

The old time tavern-keeper generally was a man of good character, respected in his community. He neither desired, nor sought promotion outside of his line of work. His aim in life was to accommodate his guests and make a comfortable living. He silently disappeared when the old fashioned way of doing things passed into limbo.

Scattered throughout Upstate New York are many of these sleepy old monuments; survivors of a bygone age, some hastening into decay; weather-beaten, neglected, solitary. Others have become pleasant rural homes, each with its own niche in history; "LaFayette stopped here."

When the railroad came thundering through, the tavern gave up in despair. It had fulfilled its mission and had written an important and colorful chapter in American history.

Chapter 5

Stagecoach Development and Travels

The first so-called stagecoaches in Upstate New York were contrivances of some local carriage or wagon-maker. As soon as wagon roads were broken through the country, the primitive "stage-waggon,"as it was called, made its appearance.

One such vehicle was owned by Samuel Stanton of Mount Pleasant, Pa. His stage, operating between Newburgh and Owego, was a three-horse lumber wagon, with hickory poles bent over to form a top, covered with canvas. Stanton made his way through the woods once a week, reaching Owego every Saturday afternoon with the mail.

Elijah Miller of Auburn, when a young man, migrated from eastern New York to Aurora, on Cayuga Lake. Reminiscing in 1835, he said he came as far as Utica in a stage "which was said to have been made by Judge William Cooper, who was the original settler of Cooperstown, and was then a member of Congress — made while he worked as a wheelwright in New Jersey. I think the stage could not have run oftener than once a week up and back from Schenectady to Utica." He mentioned the bridge over the Mohawk River had washed out a short time before, "and we came across in a scow."

The "stage-waggon" and somewhat smaller "coachee" preceded the more common and mass produced stage-coach by many years. These vehicles, in use throughout the country, were all of the same general design. Exactly when these crude coaches first emerged is uncertain. But

36

The primitive "stage-waggon" was the predecessor of the more modern stage-coach of later years. There were no doors on the sides, and consequently passengers had to climb in from the front.

as early as 1767 a "stage-chaise" was operating between Salem and Boston, Mass., while "stage-coaches" and "stage-waggons" were on the shorter routes out of Boston. In 1772 a "stage-chariot" was on the road between Boston and Marblehead, Mass.

Following the Revolution, staging advanced westward into New York State, and familiar "stage-waggon" woodcuts adorned advertisements as early as 1795.

The body of the "stage-waggon" was rather long in proportion to its breadth and contained four seats, each holding three passengers. They all sat facing the horses and driver. From the height of the seats there were no solid panels. The roof was supported by slender shafts rising up at the corners and sides. In wet weather a leather apron was folded down at the sides and back, and fastened with buttons. The curtain in the front separated the driver from the passengers, thus in bad weather, the passengers could see nothing.

The wagon had no door and the passengers climbed in through the front, stepping over the seats as they went to the end of the wagon. The driver sat on the front seat with a passenger on either side. Heavier boxes and trunks were fastened behind a frame, while smaller articles and the mail bags were stuffed under the seats, to the great annoyance of the passengers, who were frequently forced to sit with their knees up to their chins. One traveler once remarked that the passengers' feet were wedged between two trunks, "where they are most lovingly compressed whenever the vehicle makes a lurch into a rut."

The body of the wagon was suspended on two leather straps as were the early stagecoaches, passing lengthwise under it and secured upon strongly-propped horizontal bars in front and behind. There were no backs on the benches to relieve passengers during a rough and fatiguing journey over a bumpy road. The first three passengers into the wagon had the advantage of resting their shaken frames on the back of the wagon.

Women were usually given these seats and it was amusing to watch them crawl over the seats. If it happened to be late they had to straddle over the men who sat in the front. This type of vehicle was still in use west of Albany in 1818.

One observer noted two classes of "stage-waggons" in use in the early days:

"The light waggons are on the same construction, and are calculated to accommodate from four to twelve people. The only difference between a small waggon and a coachee is, that the latter is better finished, has varnished panels, and doors at the side. The former has no doors, but the passengers scramble in the best way they can, over the seat of the driver. The waggons are used universally for stage carriages."

Stories were frequently told of the driver requesting passengers to lean out of the carriage, first to one side then the other, to prevent the stage from overturning in deep ruts. But contradicting the frequency of accidents, another traveler noted in 1807: "Though the roads are in general very bad, yet the clumsy waggon is proportionably strong to encounter the shocks; and accidents but rarely happen."

Eventually this stage-waggon was replaced by a new model of coach which had but three seats and a door at the side. The driver's seat was outside and entirely separate from the interior. Passengers seated in the front faced the rear. On the New York to Albany route there was a locked box under the seat for the through mail. Only the postmasters at each end had keys. This type of coach was encouraged by the Post Office Department and had been designed especially for the department by Levi Pease, proprietor of a stage line between New York and Boston.

The newer coaches in use on the Hudson Valley route were built either in Wilmington, Delaware, or Newark, New Jersey. But it was only natural that Albany and Troy would become centers of stagecoach manufacturing. In Albany, it was the factory of the Goold's, established by James Goold in 1813. This firm built the stagecoach bodies, which, it was said, when placed on iron wheels, were used as the cars on the first train on the Mohawk & Hudson Railroad between Albany and Schenectady.

The manufacture of carriages and coaches was one of Troy's early industries. In May, 1815, Veazie & Bernard were building these vehicles, in a two-story wooden building. Thomas Williams joined the company in 1818. Charles Veazie remained in business until 1836.

Orasmus Eaton began making coaches and carriages in 1820. In 1836 he and Uri Gilbert formed a partnership and continued this line of business until their factory was destroyed by fire in 1852. The *Troy Sentinel,* on May 8, 1827, reviewed the changes made in the construction of carriages, for the conveyance of travelers:

"The improvement in the mode of conveyance in this country is not confined to steamboats and the water, as those may well testify who recollect the difference be-

This is the typical, bone-jolting manufactured "Troy Coach" that plied the old turnpikes of Upstate New York in the 1820s. There was only one door through which nine passengers entered; three in each seat. Baggage was carried in the "boot" in the rear, or under the driver's box. *(Onondaga Historical Association)*

tween our light, elegant and convenient stage-coaches, with their spring seats and easy motion, and the lumbering vehicles which were in use for the purpose some twelve or fifteen years ago. We are happy to know that the public are indebted to the ingenuity and enterprise of citizens of Troy for some of these additional conveniences.

"The valuable improvement of fixing a seat over the baggage and a railing around the top of the carriage was introduced, we believe, by Mr. Charles Veazie of this city; and one of the elegant stage-coaches lately turned out from the shop of O. Eaton, we notice a still further improvement of a similar kind. An extra seat is placed on the top of the coach, just behind the seat of the drivers. It is thus fixed in a more pleasant and agreeable situation, and gives, at the same time, a better balance to the load."

In 1830, about 50 post coaches and 100 other carriages, valued at about $50,000, were made at the works of Charles Veazie and Orasmus Eaton. "Eaton and Veazie have rendered Trojan carriages almost as noted as the wooden horse of old Troy," commended the *Troy Budget* in 1831. "Their coaches are sent to all parts of the Union and are everywhere noted for their superior beauty and utility."

Troy coaches were then in use of the National Road, on the stage lines of the southern and into the expanding West. Everywhere they were recognized as the best. The 1840s were busy years for Eaton & Gilbert. By 1850 some 5,000 of their coaches were in use throughout North America.

Eaton & Gilbert rebuilt their factory after the fire, but turned their attention to building railroad and street cars. Abbott & Downing of Concord, New Hampshire, filled the void of stagecoach manufacture; meeting the demands of an expanding western frontier with their famed "Concord Coach."

Horatio Gates Spafford, author of numerous tour guides and Gazeteers, in 1815, wrote a small monograph called *Some Cursory Observations on the Construction of Wheel-Carriages*. Regarding stagecoaches, he said: the wobbling motion which on rough and stony roads constantly threw the wheels to the right and left, was caused by the height of the load, raised above the center of the wheels.

He said the higher the load was raised, the greater and more violent was the motion, and the greater the friction and loss of propelling power. "Stages for passengers, and pleasure carriages, which have their loads thus raised, sustain a very great loss in this way, besides the increased inconvenience, and danger of upsetting. If, therefore, these premises be correct, there will be great advantage in these respects also, by suspending the load in the way I propose, below, rather than above the centre of the wheels."

He continued: "The very great increase of travelling by Stages in the United States, within a few years past, has given an increased importance to the enquiry, whether or not the construction and form of these vehicles be susceptible of improvement? I think they may be very essentially improved; and certainly, without resorting to any new invention, they may at least be made much easier draught, and far more secure from the danger of upsetting. Nor ought it to be unworthy of consideration, that the labor may be made far less cruely severe upon the thousands of poor animals that are every year worn out in drawing them."

The stagecoaches operating on the "Old Line" between Albany and Buffalo weighed about 2,400 pounds. Of this vehicle, Captain Basil Hall, an English visitor to the United States, wrote in 1830: "The American Mail Stage in which we journeyed over so many as well as civilized regions, deserves a place at our hands. The springs, it will be observed, are of hide, like those of the French Diligence — and everything about it is made of the strongest materials. There is only one door, by which the nine passengers enter the vehicle, three for each seat, the centre sufferers placing themselves on a movable bench, with a broad leather band to support their backs. Instead of panels, these Stages are fitted with leather curtains. The baggage is piled behind, or is thrust into the boot in front. They carry no outside passengers — and indeed it would try the nerves as well as the dexterity of the most harlequin that ever preserved his balance, not to be speedily pitched to the ground from the top of an American coach, on almost any road that I had the good fortune to travel over in that country."

THE OLD STAGE-COACH

The rude rugged bridges all growled at the stage,
The rough rolling ridges all gave it a lift,
You read of the route like the line of a page,
When dropped out of day into twilight and rift!
Through the sloughs of October it heavily rolled
And lurched like a ship that is mounting a sea,

O'er settling macadams on torrents untold.
Now in silence and sand midway up to the knee
It visioned the night with its yellow-eyed lamps,
Like creatures that prowl out of gunshot of camps,
When plunging along through the gloom of the swamps
With bolt, jolt and thump and the driver's "Ahoy"!
It struck with a bounce on the ribbed corduroy.
And from hemlock to hemlock long in and log out,
The coach jumped and jounced in a trip-hammer bout,
Through Gothic old chams that swallowed the night
Out into the clearings all golden with light;
Where flocks of white villages lay in the grass,
And watched for the stage and its cargo to pass.

Many European tourists took the stagecoach on their journey across New York State. Although they were impressed with the varied scenery, their comments regarding stage travel were not generally complimentary.

The accounts often are spiced with personal observations of traveling conditions of those times. Travelers unaccustomed to American roads often became inflicted with what local gentry called "stage pukes." Often the stage was overcrowded; making it extremely uncomfortable, especially over long distances. Following are three contemporary accounts of stage travel. The first is from Captain Barclay's *Agricultural Tour in the United States and Canada*; a trip made in May, 1841, from Albany to Niagara Falls.

"The American stage-coach is a most ungainly vehicle, carrying nine inside, three on a front seat, three on a back seat, and three on a bench hung in the middle; instead of panels, it has oil-skin curtains to shut down at night; its body is something in the form of a boat, resting on strong leather slings instead of steel springs, which indeed would not stand a mile on their roads; it consequently dances in the air like a balloon, giving a certain kind of variety to the monotony of a journey. The coachman sits on a bench, considerably lower than the horses,

Changes and improvements in the construction and design of stagecoaches are exemplified in these two old prints from an old history of Albany.

and there being no pad-terrets the reins dangle loose and afford no command of the horses; but they are so admirably broken that, although fine high-spirited animals, they regulate their pace instantly at his call.

"This was the first trial I had had of an American stage-coach, and I sincerely hope it may be the last, until the means of conducting them with the infliction of less torture on passengers be devised, as certainly a more abominable conveyance than this vehicle, or roads more abominable than those it was dragged over, can hardly be imagined.

"Each man drives a twelve or fifteen mile stage, and what much surprised me, pulls up every four or five miles and gives his horses an ad libitum dose of water. Including the long delays in changing horses, dining, breakfasting, &c. the average speed does not exceed four miles an hour. The coachees are paid by the proprietors at the rate of twelve dollars per month and receive no fee from passengers; and this latter is the rule also with all public servants in the States, as in hotels, steam-boats, and railways.

"My anticipations, it may be supposed, were none of the most pleasurable, when in one of the vehicles I have endeavoured to describe, I found myself placed beside eight large men and a child. For a time I submitted to threatened suffocation added to the risk of dislocated joints, but soon finding my position no longer endurable I tried what effect the offer of a fee would have in inducing the American coachee to favour me with a seat beside himself; for outsiders, no doubt from a regard for people's bones, are not here encouraged. A fee had the same virtue with him as it has in such quarters in other parts of the world, and accordingly mounted the bench, beside the driver whom I found of an injocose and taciturn class, thankful enough for information as to foreign modes but not themselves of a communicative turn.

"I still however underwent a course of excrutiating jolting, and was exposed to continual danger of dislocation of my joints, or of being pitched off; but I enjoyed the free air of Heaven, and what to me was for the time of more importance, a full view of the country than which nothing can be imagined more beautiful. Composed of alternating hill and dale it strongly reminded me of the most admired parts of Northamptonshire; but although all cleared and enclosed, the land evidently is mismanaged and much of its intrinsic value thereby lost.

"We changed horses at Geneva, twenty-three miles from Auburn and delightfully situate on the lake of that name, forty miles in length and three in breadth. It is surrounded by a country possessing that indescribable beauty and richness which characterize the finest districts of this part of America."

Upon leaving Canandaigua, Captain Barclay, "having as I felt quite enough of an American stage-coach," hired a phaeton to convey him to Genesee. Another Englishman, Frederick Fitzgerald DeRoos, had these words for the American stagecoach.

"At four o'clock in the morning we again set off, and, as much rain had fallen in the night, the roads were in a dreadful state. The coach company now consisted of nine passengers inside, one on the top; (which from its convex form is a very precarious situation) and three on the box, besides the coachman, who sat on the knees of the unfortunate middle man — an uneasy burthen, considering the intense heat of the weather.

"It matters little to the American driver where he sits; he is indeed in all respects a far different personage from his great-coated prototype in England. He is in general extremely dexterious in the art of driving, though his costume is of a most grotesque description. Figure to yourself of a slipshod sloven, dressed in a stupid calico jacket, and an old straw hat, alternately arranging the fragile harness of his horses, and springing again upon his box with surprising agility; careless of the bones of his passengers and confident in his skill and resources, he scruples not frequently to gallop his coach over corduroy roads (so called from being formed of the trunks of trees laid transversely), or dash it around corners, and through holes that would appal the heart of the stoutest English coachman, however elated with gin, or initiated by opposition.

"I was once whirled along one of these roads, when the leathers (barbarous substitutes for springs), which supported the carriage gave way with a sudden shock. The undaunted driver instantly sprang from his box, tore a stake from a rail fence by the road side, laid it across the body of the coach, and was off again before I had properly recovered the use of my senses, which were completely bewildered by the jolting I had undergone.

"I can compare it to nothing but the tub of Regulus without the nails. When the lash and bull-end of the whip fail him, he does not scruple to use his foot as the situation of his seat allows the application of it to his wheelers.

"The manners of my companions in the coach were rude and coarse. There was, however, a kindness and cordiality about them which pierced through their rough exterior, and reconciled me insensibly to their company. They always designated me as 'the Englishman'."

Frances Trollope was very critical of American stagecoach travel in her 1832 volume, *Domestic Manners of Americans*. In June, 1828, she jounced eastward across New York State, complaining all the way. The coach had stopped in Vernon to take in a "lady," and when she entered, she completely filled the last vacant inch of the coach, already well filled by eight persons.

"But no sooner was she seated than her beau came forward with a most enormous wooden best-bonnet box. He paused for a while to meditate the possibilities — raised it, as if to place it on our laps — sunk it, as if to put it beneath our feet. Both alike appeared impossible; when, in true Yankee style, he addressed one of our party with, 'If you'll just step out a minute, I guess I'll find room for it.'

'Perhaps so. But how shall I find room for myself afterwards?'

"This was uttered in European accents, and in an instant half a dozen whiskey drinkers stepped from the whiskey store, and took the part of the beau.

'That's because you'll be English travellers, I expect; but we have travelled in better countries than Europe— we have travelled in America—and the box will go, I calculate.'

"We remonstrated on the evident injustice of the proceeding, and I ventured to say that, as we had none of us any luggage in the carriage because space was so very small, I thought a chance passenger could have no right so greatly to incommodoe us.

"During this contest the coachman sat upon the box without saying a word, but seemed greatly to enjoy the joke; the question of the box, however, was finally decided in our favour by the nature of human material, which cannot be compressed beyond a certain degree."

In de Veaux's amusing and interesting guide to Saratoga Springs, Niagara Falls and Canada (published in Buffalo in 1841) he gives some interesting suggestions to prospective travelers which throw light upon the difficulties of travel in the early days.

Of stagecoaches, he wrote: "Of these old-fashioned conveyances little need be said. Ladies are always accommodated with the back seat. The middle seat is the easiest, the front seat the best to sleep on; but if you are subject to sickness when riding, always avoid it. Post coaches, if not crowded with too many passengers, over good roads, in fair weather, afford the most safe and agreeable mode of transit of any other; but the flyaway character of travelers is fast driving them out of use. From these vehicles the scenery of the country can always be advantageously viewed; and as the wheels roll on, the hours pass in social chat, free remark, amusing anecdotes and gay sallies, often truly pleasant and interesting."

Chapter 6

Canandaigua – A Stagecoach Town

"Though I have mentioned the lake first, the little town of Canandaigua precedes it, in returning from the west. It is as pretty a village as ever man contrived to build. Every house is surrounded by an ample garden, and at that flowery season, they were half buried in roses.

"It is true these houses are of wood, but they are so neatly painted, in such perfect repair, and show so well within their leafy setting, that it is impossible not to admire them." — *Domestic Manners of Americans* by Frances Trollope, London, 1832.

Canandaigua, its broad main street lined with elegant homes surrounded by spacious gardens, was the stage-coach center of the "western country" for more than three decades. From here, stage routes radiated in all directions.

As early as 1805 it was the western terminus of a weekly line of stages linking the western frontier settlements with Albany. Two years later, with the improvement of roads, John Metcalf was granted an exclusive franchise to operate stages between Canandaigua and Buffalo.

Canandaigua was an impressive place with its over-powering atmosphere of great wealth, law and learning. The older families with their long New England pedigrees were regarded as aristocrats of fabulous wealth. There was an air about this well-groomed village placing it far above the normal cut of pioneer settlements.

The traveler passing down Main Street in the coach

"Blossom's" Hotel in Canandaigua was a noted rendezvous point on the great western stage route in the palmy days of land travel.

bound for Blossom's Hotel took particular note of the fine Georgian architecture standing back from the curb in well-kept grounds with box-bordered walks. Here and there was a white or buff-colored law office, with a brass knocker on the door.

The courthouse corner was a beehive of lawyers. On summer afternoons the young gentlemen could be seen reading under the trees. Such notable residents as Gideon and Francis Granger (Postmasters-General under Madison in 1812 and Harrison in 1840) might be seen walking down the street in cloak and broadcloth.

Blossom's Hotel, on a bluff with a commanding view of the community, was a commodious brick structure built in 1815 by Belah D. Coe, one of the "Old Line" proprietors. William Blossom was its proprietor after 1824. Before the railroad came it was the center of travel.

It had a peaked roof with great chimneys coming up from the spits and ovens. Through the dark archway the stage-coach would emerge.

Blossom's was the best hostelry in the town, where the notables of the day came to take the stage for Albany or Washington. It reflected the era of ruffled shirts and gold-headed canes. When the nabobs gathered at Blossom's, the harness brasses and coach varnish got an extra rubbing. The horses were a bit fresher and the driver a prouder man to be carrying important personages.

Before the restless horses got away to the music of the stage-horn, there was a shaking of hands and doffing of beaver hats. A bell atop the hotel regulated most of the affairs of the village. The proprietor was a man of fine appearance and his suavity of manners established his wide reputation as a landlord.

Canandaigua's growth as a center of business and legal life is attributed to its being the seat of the affairs of Phelps and Gorham's Purchase. Its fortunes were built on land speculation and day-to-day prosperity was measured on the number of deeds filed in the county clerk's office. It could be said that Canandaigua did a "land office business."

There were eleven attorneys registered in Canandaigua as early as 1810. Preceding Blossom's in prominence as a "stage-house" was Taylor's Hotel, an old rookery built in 1796 as the Dudley Tavern. On July 26, 1810, DeWitt Clinton, one-time Governor of New York State, noted that Taylors was "an indifferent house," alluding to poor accommodations. But even at this early date, Clinton said, "the main street strikes the outlet of the lake at right angles, and has a great many elegant houses."

Upon passing the local coachmaker's shop, Clinton notices a "plain coachee with leather curtains" belonging to Jemima Wilkinson, in for repairs. Clinton said there was a curious inscription on the back, in large letters, V*F. The prophetess, he noted, resided with 30 or 40 followers at Crooked Lake, some 25 miles to the southeast.

"The Old Stage and Turnpike." From a drawing by W. L. Taylor.
(Copyright 1900 by the Curtis Publishing Company)

"She is opposed to war, to oaths, and to marriage; and to her confidential friends she represents herself as Jesus Christ personified in the body of Jemima Wilkinson."

Clinton spent the night with a friend, John C. Spencer, one of the most prominent political figures in the state in his time; who, during his illustrious career, had served as Secretary of War.

Like so many towns of its day, the number of taverns was out of proportion to its size. There were "by far too many taverns and groceries (as there are every where in such places)," Horatio Gates Spafford noted in his 1824 *Gazeteer of the State of New York.* Accommodations for travelers, even in such a place with the great profusion of taverns, often left much to be desired; even in elegant Canandaigua.

Elkanah Watson, noted advocate of internal improvements, found that signing his name to the register bought him little more than space on the floor. On an overnight stop in Canandaigua in 1819, Watson found that "The public hotel was bad, the house full, and myself, at the age of sixty, compelled to lie upon a buffalo robe in the third story, in place of a bed."

Watson noted the village contained many splendid residences, "and a wealthy and genteel population. Here resides Gideon Granger, the late Post-Master General, and eminent for his lofty and diversified intellectual endowments."

Stagecoach service in and out of Canandaigua developed rapidly after the War of 1812. A tri-weekly mail stage left the village for the west starting in 1814. Service commenced July 20, 1815, via Geneva and Auburn; went through to Utica in two days. E. B. Dewey was proprietor and seats were obtainable at Coe's Stage House, later Blossom's.

Bi-weekly service to Rochester was inaugurated January 4, 1816, by Samuel Hildreth. By August, 1817, additional service was running between Canandaigua and Rochester, via East Bloomfield, Mendon and Pittsford. Oliver Phelps of Ludlowville, near Ithaca, established a line of tri-weekly stages in May, 1818, between Newburgh and Canandaigua; the trip being accomplished in three days.

William Faulkner of Geneva and W. W. Fenlon of Montezuma commenced their daily line between Canandaigua and Montezuma in August, 1822. Coaches would meet the steamboat "Enterprise" at Cayuga, and the Packetboat "Echo" on the Erie Canal at Montezuma; leaving Gooding's Tavern in Canandaigua at 9 A.M.

The growth of the stagecoach business was quite noticeable in the 1820s; contrary to a theory voiced by many historians that packetboats on the Erie Canal made this mode of travel obsolete. In 1826, eighty stages arrived and

NEW DAILY LINE OF STAGES.

From New-York to Buffalo, by the way of Ithaca and Geneva.

THIS line will leave New-York every day, Sundays excepted, and run through Newark, Springfield, Bottle-Hill, Morristown, Succasunny-Plains, Newton, Milford and Dundaff, three times a week by the way of Chenango Point, and three times a week by the way of Montrose, to Owego, and from thence daily, by the way of Ithaca and Ovid, to Geneva, where it intersects a daily line to Canandaigua, Rochester, Buffalo, Lewiston, &c.

Returning, will leave Geneva at the same times, and pursue the same routes to New-York. At Mott's, New-Milford, this line intersects the Newburgh line, which runs from thence, three times a week, to Newburgh.

The importance of this line to the public will readily be seen: It opens a direct communication between the city of New York and the western part of the state, through New Jersey and the northern section of Pennsylvania. At Newton, (N. J.) it intersects a line which has recently been established from that place to Philadelphia, three times a week. At Montrose, it intersects the line to Wilkesbarre, Harrisburgh, &c. At Chenango Point, it intersects a line which runes north, thro' Greene, Oxford, &c. to Utica, and intersects the Albany line by Cooperstown and Cherry Valley, at Sherburne. At Owego, it intersects a line which runs through Tioga Point, Elmira, &c. to Bath. Thus affording an opportunity to gentlemen who are wishing to travel in either of those directions, a cheap and expeditious mode of conveyance. The accommodations are good,—the distance is less, and the fare much lower, than on any other route from New York to Geneva.

Good Horses and Coaches, and careful, attentive drivers, are engaged, and every attention will be paid by the Proprietors, to the comfort and safety of Passengers.

Seats may be taken at J. Patten's, 71 Cortland street, New York; at I. I. Roy's, Jersey City; Bawle's Tavern, Newark; at the Hotel, Dundaff; Buckingham's, Montrose; Robinson's Hotel, Chenango Point; either of the public houses in Owego; Ithaca Hotel, and at Grant's Coffee House, Ithaca; and at Faulkner's Hotel, Geneva.

S. HEMENWAY,
ISAAC POST,
I. I. ROY,
I. MOTT, *and others.*

42tf

LOOK AT THIS!

A STAGE leaves Canandaigua *every day,* for Utica, at the following rates of Fare:

	$ cts.
From Canandaigua to Geneva,	75
to Cayuga,	1 50
to Auburn,	2 00
to Onondaga,	2 25
to Manlius,	3 75
to Utica,	5 50
From Cayuga to Utica,	4 00
" Auburn to Utica,	3 50

J. M. SHERWOOD.

Canandaigua, Sept. 7, 1820.   3w27

Old advertisements from newspapers show extent of stagecoach business in early Canandaigua.

departed Canandaigua weekly. "The number of these vehicles, for the conveyance of passengers, increases late with astonishing rapidity," reported the *Ontario Repository*, the village newspaper, on June 28, 1826. The numerous "extras" also were well-patronized.

C. H. Coe & Co. commenced staging on January 1, 1826. The firm consisted of the brothers, Chauncey and Belah D. Coe, and Samuel Greenleaf. The partnership lasted until the death of Chauncey Coe in 1835, and was then purchased by Asa Nowlen of Avon. Thereafter, the firm was known as S. Greenleaf & Co.

An advertisement in the *Ontario Repository* of May 10, 1826, alludes to the Coes' connection with the "Old Line" proprietors:

Three Daily Lines of Coaches,
Leave the regular Mail Coach office, Blossom's Hotel, Canandaigua, for Utica.
The Eagle Coach, at 4 A.M.
" Mail   do   10 do
" Pilot, in the afternoon
Also, Two Coaches a day from the above Office, for Buffalo, and two for Rochester
Mail for Buffalo, 2 P.M.
Pilot " do   Evening
Pilot for Rochester, 4 A.M.
Mail " do   2 P.M.
May 10, 1826   C. H. Coe & Co.
Extras furnished for any of the above routes at short notice.

The year 1826 also saw the establishment of a weekly stage between Perry and Fredonia, intersecting a line between Canandaigua and Warsaw. Lawrence Lynch and others advertised three daily lines of coaches in July 1826, called the "Union Line" for Utica, Albany and Buffalo; as well as a run to Rochester. Lynch had recently taken over the tavern in Canandaigua "a little south of the new Court-House, and has fitted it up in genteel style. From his acquaintance with the travelling public in Auburn and Geneva, he hopes to receive a liberal share of the patronage."

Tri-weekly service started in May, 1827, from Canandaigua, via Rushville, Naples and Conhocton (later Cohocton), leaving Lynch's Tavern at 5 A.M. Monday, Wednesday and Friday. Returning, the stage left Bath Tuesday, Thursday and Saturday. At Conhocton, connections could be made for Dansville and Prattsburgh. Still another line operated Monday and Thursday between Canandaigua and Pen Yan. A Canandaigua newspaper editor commented "thus are the public accommodated with stages running in almost every direction, to and from this place."

In July, 1827, service was started from Canandaigua to Moscow, via Bristol, Richmond and Livonia. The line extended on from Perry to Buffalo, three times a week, and Pierpont, Frost & Co. were the proprietors.

Such a multiplicity of stagecoaches converging on Canandaigua simultaneously had its effects on a confused English traveler in the early 1830s: "When we arrived at Canandaigua, there was a great confusion in consequence of four or five stages being at the door at the same time. As they were going in different directions, the passengers were hunting for the agent, and the agent for the passengers. After the bustle had ceased and I had seen my luggage properly stowed away, I observed to the agent, that it would save much trouble and prevent mistakes, if the names of the places were put upon the coaches, as is done in France and England. His reply was the same as I uniformly received on similar occasions: 'very likely, but we have different customs here,' as if I wanted to be informed of the very thing my suggestion implied."

The staging business continued to thrive, with Canandaigua the hub of a vast network of lines, until completion of the Auburn & Rochester Railroad in 1841. Shortly before the demise of the stagecoach, Samuel Greenleaf helped establish a stage driver's reading room and library for his employees.

The rather unique effort was salutary, and characterized a God-send to the drivers. The group was known as the Canandaigua Stage Drivers Library and Reading-room Association. Dues were 12½ cents a month; the proceeds from which were used to purchase books and periodicals. Articles of association were drawn up January 1, 1839, with Steven S. Austin, President; George B. Hotchkiss, Vice-President, and Perry G. Wadhams, Librarian. On June 4, 1840, Mr. Greenleaf presented a handsome whip to the driver who had read the most Bible scripture during the past year.

The palmy days when Blossom's was a famous stagehouse, where crowds gathered to see the arrival of the four-horse post coaches, disappeared with the coming of the railroad. No longer did weary teams, aroused to a "second wind," wheel into position before the tavern door.

The famous hotel burned to the ground on December 23, 1851, and was replaced by a more commodious but less colorful Canandaigua Hotel, the following year. Ironically, this structure also was destroyed by fire on March 29, 1971, with a heavy loss of life.

The heritage that Canandaigua retains from stagecoach days lives in the many fine old residences and buildings so often remarked of in travelers' accounts. They stand in a fine state of preservation.

The old town today above the railroad tracks is like an old man in silk stockings and ruffled shirt, leaning on a gold-headed cane, contemplating the past. He is eminently respectable, an aristocrat to his finger-tips. He is proud to think he has had a hand in the building of a nation.

Chapter 7

The Era of the Drover

A story is told by old-timers along the old Seneca Turnpike of a wager once made between two drovers. The turkey drover was sure his long-legged, quick-stepping birds would win. But the more experienced drover of geese knew better.

As evening approached, the high-stepping turkeys, although far out-distancing the plodding geese, would move no farther, and roosted on the fences and in the trees for the night. No amount of persuasion could coax them to go on. Soon, the geese came plodding by. The geese driver collected his bet and went off into the night.

In the early days before railroads were established, the rutted turnpikes and state roads of New York State were thronged with droves of not only geese and turkeys, but cattle, sheep, hogs and horses as well. The drovers shared the roads with the stagecoaches, covered wagons, tinkers, peddlers, and people on foot. While the stream of covered wagons was generally west, there was a steady eastward flow of both drovers and freight wagons.

The drover has earned only an occasional mention by some local historian. Occasionally, there is an elderly local native who can relate a tale or two about drovers— not usually from his own memory, but perhaps from an antecedent. J. Reynolds Wait of Auburn, whose palatial country home on the citys western outskirts faces the old Seneca Turnpike, noted how the droves were as wide as fence to fence and the roadsides were completely free of grass and other vegetation.

Cattle, sheep, hogs and birds were driven hundreds of miles from Ohio and the midwest to Albany, New England, New York City and other centers of commerce.

In its November, 1852, issue, the *Wool Grower and Stock Register* recorded: "In years back, before the construction of railroads, the driving of cattle was a large and tedious business, the journey often extending over hundreds of miles. From this State they were generally driven to New York, Brighton and Philadelphia on the old turnpikes; during the fall, the droves used to extend for miles and public farms with pastures for Cattle as well as food and drink for the drivers were to be found within sight of each other.

"The loss on the cattle driven to market, depended of course very much on the traveling, the quality and quantity of the feed, and the care exercised in driving. But these old times have passed away and the occasion for long journeys either for men or cattle by land, no longer exists."

This and other evidence indicates farmers along the main roads rented their pastures for cattle and catered to the drovers. There are many old farm-houses which have a local reputation of having once been drovers' inns. Still other locations, such as a flat area adjacent to a stream were overnight rest stops for weary man and beast.

Typical of those who catered to drovers was Hezekiah Bowen, Jr., on the north branch of the Seneca Turnpike near Auburn. His great-grandson, Albert J. Bowen, has an old account book with one section titled "Account of Pasturing Drovers."

In late winter and early spring, before pastures were green, corn was sold to drovers in huge amounts. From Bowen's record book, 5,620 hogs passed eastward to market in about two and a half months, probably to Albany, and Bowen sold the drovers 715 bushels of corn at a price averaging 25 cents a bushel.

Turnpike tolls under the category of drovers were usually established by the laws incorporating the companies. The Seneca Road Company was incorporated by the State Legislature by an act passed April 1, 1800. For every score of cattle, a charge of six cents was levied on the drovers. Every score of sheep or hogs was three cents, and the same in proportion for a greater or lesser number.

To avoid this cost, drovers often used secondary and parallel roads which was referred to as "shunpiking." It is said that drovers often avoided the heavily traveled turnpikes as hard-packed roads were hard on the feet of the animals.

In the winter of 1846-47 a large drove of cattle was driven across Cayuga Lake on the ice to avoid the tariff on the Cayuga Bridge. The ice broke beneath the weight of the animals, and 50 head were drowned. Some that were pulled out not quite dead were killed and barrelled —and helped to fill a contract for meat for the Army.

Occasional newspaper classified advertisements note strayed cattle from passing droves, and offer a reward for their return. In the early days, local communities maintained "pounds" in which lost cattle were corraled at the expense of the owners.

The main thoroughfares of the drovers, east and west, are presently portions of Routes 5 and 20 between Albany and Buffalo; Route 80 portions of the old Hamilton & Skaneateles Turnpike, as well as other roads criss-crossing the state. But in many cases, drovers preferred to avoid the heavily-traveled stage roads with the constant oncoming traffic.

Of all the animals driven on the roads, turkeys were by far the hardest animals to handle because of their chicken-like excitability and tendency to panic and run wild. The birds were collected during the fall and brought into the villages by the farmers, and sold to the drovers.

When a sufficient number had been accumulated, the drove was started on its eastward trek, and the roads were virtually black with turkeys. Before starting on their way, the turkeys' feet were tarred as this was the most venerable part of their body. It also kept them on the road.

To prevent them from flying and consequently losing them enroute, their wings were clipped. A drover usually followed his flock wagon to care for any stray birds. The wagon carried the necessary victuals for man and beast.

A drover might employ from four to six men or boys as drivers. They were equipped with long birch rods to which were attached long leather thongs to poke the birds back into the roadway. The drivers traveled by foot at the sides of the flocks to keep them aligned.

The farms which catered to drovers and provided overnight lodgings were provided with corrals containing roosts, as turkeys must roost high to keep their feet dry and to protect them from predatory animals. Skunks especially found them juicy morsels.

These pens were stocked with feed and had water troughs. Turkeys also had to be kept well fed enroute to prevent them from losing too much weight. Corn was strewed along the road and the turkeys in that way were coaxed along. Turkey driving was slow and tedious, the average speed being seven to 10 miles a day, depending on the size of the flock and the weather. A man on horseback rode in front of the flock, scattering corn in a trail of kernels which the birds unerringly followed all day.

There are indications of cattle droves in Upstate New York as early as the 1780s. In the summer of 1787, Silas Hopkins of Lewiston, N.Y., started from New Jersey, assisting his father in driving cattle to Niagara.

"I came out twice the next summer with father upon the same business," Hopkins wrote. "Upon one of these occasions, I went with my father to the residence of Col. Butler near Newark (Niagara). He was then about fifty-five or sixty years old; had a large, pretty well cultivated farm; was living a quiet farmer's life. He was hospitable and agreeable, and I could hardly realize that he had been a leader of the Rangers. (Col. Butler died, 1794).

"In all my journeyings in those early days we were well treated by the Indians. They had a custom of levying a tribute upon all droves, by selecting a beeve from each drove as they passed through their principal towns. This they regarded as equivalent for a passage through their territories; and the drovers found it the best way to submit without murmuring."

After the coming of the railroads with their obvious alvantages of speed and handling, droving became a thing of the past. By the 1850s, the Erie and New York Central Railroads were transporting most of the livestock.

Jason Parker was the pioneer stage proprietor in the Mohawk Valley and father of the "Old Line Mail." He started his career as a mail carrier.

Chapter 8

Jason Parker – Patriarch of the "Old Line"

One day a man stopped by the stage office in Utica to apply for a job as a driver. Jason Parker said he was looking for an experienced reinsman. The man claimed previous experience on New England roads.

Parker led the man outside and told him, "there's a team and coach in the yard; you may drive me to Whitesboro." This was about five miles from Utica. The driver mounted the box and Parker climbed inside. Being somewhat of a rogue, the driver struck every stone in the road to and from Whitesboro.

Upon their return, Parker told the man: "If you can hit all the stones in the road, you can miss them; I will hire you." This is one of the old stories told of the most celebrated of the "Old Line" stage proprietors.

A native of Adams, Massachusetts, Parker settled in nearby New Hartford in 1790, shortly after his marriage to Roxanna Day. Here he cleared two farms in pioneer fashion, but before long had to give up this vocation because of his health.

Parker moved to Old Fort Schuyler (later Utica) in 1794 and undertook the duties of post-rider between Canajoharie and Whitestown. Being proficient in his work, Parker soon was given the mail contract. His journeys were made on horseback and occasionally on foot. At times, Mrs. Parker assisted her husband in pick up and delivery.

The first action to extend the stagecoach business westward from Albany was made by Moses Beal, a Schenectady innkeeper, in 1793. He established a weekly service between Albany and Canajoharie. His local rival in the tavern business, John Hudson, soon placed a competing line on the road between Albany and Schenectady. In 1794, after a period of competition, an agreement was reached by which Hudson would control the Albany-Schenectady business, and Beal between Schenectady and Canajoharie. Parker continued up the Mohawk Valley to Utica.

Extending stagecoach service west of Albany had been discussed as early as 1790. Elkanah Watson, a staunch advocate of internal improvements as the means of developing a new nation, wrote:

"Some facts within my personal knowledge connected with the establishment of the first public conveyance west of Albany, I think worthy of notice, as they, with singular force, exhibit the progress of improvement.

"On our return from this expedition (into the western part of the state), Mr. Van Rensselaer and myself arrived at Schenectady on the evening of the 10th of October (1791) and proceeded from the bateau to the tavern of Mr. Hudson. We were naturally, after an absence of six weeks, extremely solicitous to reach our families. Mr. Hudson made every effort in his power during the evening to secure us suitable conveyance to Albany the ensuing day, but without success. He at length informed us that there was no possible way of getting to Albany, except by riding on a load of shingles, or to go with a pair of half-broke colts.

"We preferred the later alternative. We urged Mr. Hudson to run a weekly stage to Albany, who seemed much disposed to embark in the enterprise, but was, he said, fearful of the result, for a Mr. Douglass had made the experiment five years before, and ruined himself, as he found no passengers to patronize him.

"In about a fortnight I met one Beal, who carried the mail once a week, usually on horseback, from Albany to

Canajoharie, which was then the frontier post-office. This weekly mail supplied the whole western territory. Such was my information. I pressed him to carry his mail in a cheap wagon, calculated to accommodate way-passengers, and gave him a letter to Mr. Hudson, urging him to unite with Beal in the measure.

"Early in December following, I was delighted to hear the sound of a stage horn, and to see Beal dashing down State-street with the Schenectady and Canajoharie mail wagon, which was announced to run once a week. In the rapid increase of the settlements in the vicinity of Whitestown, they soon found abundant encouragement.

"To this humble experiment may be traced the foundation of the immense and splendid stage organization which now connects Albany with the teaming regions of the west. Perhaps the annals of the world does not exhibit in such a department a progress so vast and wonderful."

After the death of John Hudson in 1795, Ananias Platt, a tavern keeper, removed from Lansingburgh to Schenectady, taking over the tavern and staging interests between Albany and Schenectady. A connecting line was established between Canajoharie and Cooperstown. In summer, a line operated between Schenectady and Ballston Springs.

Advertisements of the "Western Mail Stages" were thereafter signed by Beal, Platt and Parker. To eliminate competition, these proprietors made an unsuccessful appeal to the State Legislature for an exclusive right on January 18, 1797, to operate stages over these routes.

Postmaster General Timothy Pickering, in a letter to Jason Parker dated September 6, 1794, wrote to accept his proposals to carry the mail between Canajoharie and Whitestown. Hudson was to carry it from Utica to Schenectady, and Beal from there to Canajoharie.

Late in 1797, after the Genesee Road had been made "fit for carriages to run through," stagecoach service was extended weekly to Geneva under the auspices of John House and Thomas Powell, inkeepers in Utica and Geneva. In 1802, House moved away from Utica and Parker inherited his business. In March, 1803, Parker and Levi Stevens of Geneva petitioned the legislature for an exclusive franchise on the route from Utica westward, which was granted the following year.

Jason Parker's stables were a few hundred feet west of the present Utica Newspapers building, in the rear of the old National Hotel. This hotel was Parker's headquarters. The stables were completely destroyed by fire on January 27, 1831.

One of Parker's early adversaries in the stagecoach business was Joshua Ostrom, who started up a line in 1810. A glance at their respective advertisments illustrates not only the rivalry and strife between proprietors, but the ensuing improvement in service as a result.

On September 20, 1810, Ostrom, Baker & Swan, and J. Wetmore & Co. announced a new 'steamboat line' of stages to leave Albany Monday and Friday, and Utica, Monday and Thursday. Six days later, Powell & Parker, Campbell & Co. ("in order to prevent the delay at Utica") in their western line, established a new daily line.

Next, Ostrom & Co. are running their line three times a week, but "without the incumbrance of post office regulations." Then on January 21, 1811, Parker & Powell advertised "Eight changes of horses. The mail stage now leaves Baggs, Utica, every morning at four o'clock. Passengers will breakfast at Maynard's, Herkimer, dine at Josiah Shepard's, Palatine, and sup (on oysters) at Thomas Powell's Tontine Coffee House, Schenectady." They further commented, "Those ladies and gentlemen who will favor this line with their patronage may be assured of having good horses, attentive drivers, warm carriages, and that there shall not be any running or racing horses on the line."

The rivals, still unencumbered by postal regulations, a week later, were prepared to "go through in one day, unless the extreme badness of the travelling render it utterly impossible." Ostrom offered passengers the liberty to breakfast, dine and sup, "where, when and on what they please."

Only one further advertisement of Ostrom and his associates appeared in the newspapers, dated April 3, 1811. He apparently was unable to compete against the Old Line of Jason Parker, and "wound up his affairs."

Parker's success in the stagecoach business was attributed to his ability to employ competent personnel. One of these was a young man named John Butterfield who was employed by Parker as a runner and driver. A runner's job was to solicit passengers from competing lines of stages, canal packets and steamboats. This occupation flourished during the stagecoach era, and to some degree after the coming of the railroads.

About 1820 a new line of competing stages was started by Peter Cole, who employed a super-politic runner named Henry S. Storms. Parker's answer was to send his agent, Theodore S. Faxton, to Albany, in search of a runner to watch the wits of Storms.

Faxton found such a person in John Butterfield, at the time a driver for "Old Line" proprietors Asa Sprague and Aaron Thorp. Butterfield's natural talent and initiative in luring passengers to Parker's stages was more than Cole could contend with, and he soon withdrew from the business.

In later years Butterfield was a founder of the American Express Company and was credited as the father of the Butterfield Overland Mail Company, known throughout the western United States as the "Butterfield Stage." Upon arriving in Utica, Butterfield drove a conveyance to the various taverns and canal boat landings to drum up trade. His first home was a small room in a dilapidated stable near the canal.

Living frugally, he saved his meager earnings while applying himself diligently to his duties. Butterfield was born November 18, 1801, on his father's farm at Berne, in the Helderberg mountains of Albany County.

Of an old New England family, young Butterfield manifested a natural fondness for horses. On occasional trading trips to Albany with his father, the boy spent his time hanging around the livery stables. Tradition states he first learned to blow a call on the post horn from one of the old Boston Mail coach drivers. No doubt these boyhood visits inspired his ambition to drive a stage.

At the age of 19, Butterfield, with his parents' consent, went to Albany to seek his fortune. Making the rounds of the livery and exchange stables, he finally obtained a job with the old established firm of Thorp & Sprague. Being an ambitious youth, he soon gained the reputation of one of the best and most reliable drivers in Albany.

After coming with Parker, Butterfield soon started his own livery business by purchasing a horse and a two-seated carriage from a traveler he met at the Canal Coffee House in Utica. Although this small venture took nearly all of his capital, he eventually built up a livery trade that rivaled the older established concerns.

He married Malinda Harriet Baker in February, 1822, and the couple opened a boarding house in connection with the livery. Butterfield's association with the Parker interests lasted until 1841, when railroads superceded stage lines. He and his partners erected the Exchange Building on the site of the old Canal Coffee House. They also controlled the Eagle Tavern and had extensive real estate holdings in Utica.

In subsequent years, Butterfield extended his interests in other business ventures. Anticipating the eventual decline in staging, he pursued the packet boat business and the growing steamer trade on the Great Lakes.

In this early period, Butterfield was ably assisted in routine office work by James V. P. Gardner, an executive of exceptional business acumen who later helped direct the affairs of Butterfield's western enterprises.

As a citizen of Utica, Butterfield labored unceasingly in arousing local interest and served as mayor in 1856. He also fostered numerous local enterprises such as railroad and street car lines and cotton mills. But he is best recalled as the dean of American expressmen.

Two other important personages in the Parker regime were Theodore S. Faxton and Silas D. Childs, both of whom joined Butterfield in many of his business pursuits. Both self-made men, their closely-paralleling careers won them permanent record in Utica's early history.

Both Faxton and Childs were natives of Conway, Mass., and were almost the same age. Both came to Utica penniless, and attained wealth and influence by middle age. After staging had ceased they both invested heavily in other modes of conveyance, and were partners in local enterprises.

Faxton came to Utica in 1812 at the age of 20. In 1813, he became a driver for Parker, and held the reins, four-in hand, continuously until 1817 when he became superintendent of the men, horses and coaches. He attended school in Clinton for a brief period, but returned to Parker's employ a short time later. Thereafter he mounted the box only on special occasions to demonstrate his skill at the reins. One of his proudest recollections was when General Lafayette passed through in June, 1825. Faxton assembled six dashing greys, harnessed them in silver plate, and drove a borrowed carriage to Whitesboro.

When Lafayette alighted from a packet boat which had brought him from Syracuse, he climbed with his party into Faxton's carriage. Faxton said he felt grander that day "than Napoleon Bonaparte."

Silas D. Childs joined the Parker firm in 1816 as a bookkeeper; the stage office then being in the southwest corner in the basement of Bagg's Hotel. He proved himself a capable worker, and in 1820, Parker took him in as a partner. Faxton also soon joined in the partnership.

Although the booking of names and filling out of way-bills was not as colorful as driving galloping horses, Childs' job as an agent was no less important in running the business.

The accomplishments of these two men in other business pursuits alone would fill a volume. But it was Parker and his stagecoach empire which started them on their long and successful careers.

One of the most memorable events in the early career of Faxton and the history of the "Old Line" was a test of speed on Saturday, February 8, 1823. Jason Parker staged the run to demonstrate the swiftness of his conveyances in covering the 192-mile round trip between Utica and Albany; a feat accomplished in 16 hours and 41 minutes.

Shortly after midnight the stagecoach pulled away from Bagg's Hotel with six passengers aboard. Arrangements had been made in advance for full relays of horses, ready and harnessed. The company breakfasted at Johnstown, arriving in Albany at 9 A.M. After an hour's rest, the stage left Albany, reaching Utica at 7:02 P.M. The running time included several changes of horses, accompanied with the delays common to stage travel.

The travelers were not content until they had eked out the full 200 miles by extending their ride to nearby New Hartford and return.

But records are made to be broken. On February 22, 1823, the Mohawkers were outdone when a party of gentlemen were conveyed in a public stage from Buffalo to Batavia and return, in five hours and 29½ minutes; a distance of 80 miles.

When stagecoaching was at its zenith, Utica saw many excellent drivers. One of the ablest and most faithful, after several years of steady service, fell in love with a buxom young widow who owned a large farm just east of the village. He offered his hand and heart, and the thrifty widow accepted, with the proviso he give up his profession and help her with the farm. He turned in his whip and horn, and married her. As a wedding gift, Parker presented the couple with an all-expense paid trip to Niagara Falls.

The second day of the driver's life as a farmer found him ploughing a field beside the turnpike with a yoke of slow-moving oxen. Soon, a stagecoach came clattering down the road. As he looked, he noticed his favorite team, four chestnut sorrels, coming into view. Their burnished coats were agleam in the sunlight and their manes tossed in the morning breeze.

The driver gave the farmer a salute on his horn. He cracked the whip over the heads of the leaders, and the horses broke into a gallop. The ploughman stopped his work. He unyoked the oxen, walked across the meadow to the house, packed his carpet bag. He stole out the back door and went straight to the stage office.

The following day he was on the box of his favorite old coach, smartly snapping his long lashed whip over the horses' heads. His wife sold the farm in Utica, and, as the stories say, lived happily ever after.

The name of Jason Parker was as synonymous with stagecoaching as Commodore Vanderbilt with railroading. At the time of Parker's death on September 28, 1830, there were eight daily lines of stages through Utica running east and west, and four lines north and south. Parker's empire also included holding major mail contracts in association with others across the state. Eighty stages arrived and departed from Utica weekly in the early 1830s.

After long and useful lives, Childs died July 11, 1866, and Faxton died on November 30, 1881.

STAGES.

J. Parker & Co. Utica, proprietors.

WESTWARD.

Pilot, for Buffalo and Lewiston, leaves daily at 6 P. M.; through in 48 hours.

Telegraph, for Buffalo, leaves daily at 2 A. M.; through in 33 hours; limited to 6 passengers.

Eclipse, for Buffalo, Rochester and Lewiston, leaves daily at 7 A. M.; limited to 8 pasengers; through in 3 days by day light.

Eagle, for Buffalo, Rochester and Lewiston, leaves daily from 10 to 12 A. M.; or on the arrival of the packets, from Schenectady.

Distance, from Utica to Rochester 140 miles. From Utica to Buffalo, 202 miles. From Buffalo to Niagara Falls 21 miles, and thence to Lewiston 7 miles.

EASTWARD.

Telegraph, for Albany leaves daily at 3 A. M.; limited to 6 inside passengers; arrives at Albany in time for the 5 o'clock P. M. steamboat, and the passengers arrive at New York in 24 hours from Utica.

Eclipse, leaves daily at 7 A. M.; through to Schenectady in 12 hours; limited to 8 passengers.

Pilot, for Albany, leaves daily at 9 P. M.; through in time for the P. M. steamboat for New York.

Distance, from Utica to Schenectady 81 miles. From Schenectady to Albany 15 miles. From Albany to New York 145 miles.

SOUTHWARD.

Mail, for Oxford and Binghamton, leaves daily, except the Sabbath, at 5 A. M.; via New Hartford, Paris, Sangerfield, Madison, Hamilton, Sherburne, Norwich, to Oxford the first day; thence through Greene to Binghamton next day at noon. From Binghamton he mail goes via Montrose to the city of Philadelphia.

Distance, from Utica to Oxford 60 miles. From Utica to Binghamton 90 miles. From Utica to Philadelphia 256 miles.

Mail, for Ithaca, leaves every Sunday, Tuesday and Thursday at 9 P. M., and arrive in less than 24 hours; via New Hartford, Clinton, Sangerfield, Madison, Eaton, Woodstock, De Ruyter, Truxton, Homer, Cortlandt and Dryden.

Distance, from Utica to Ithaca (south-west) 96 miles.

☞ Extra coaches, with regular relays of horses, furnished at all times for Niagara Falls and Trenton Falls.

John Butterfield, Utica, proprietor.

SOUTHWARD.

For Cooperstown, daily, except the Sabbath; leaves at 7 A. M., Monday, Wednesday and Friday via Richfield Springs; and Tuesday, Thursday and Saturday via Burlington.

Distance, from Utica to Canadaraga Springs in Richfield 30 miles. From Utica to Cooperstown 46 miles.

For Mount Pleasant, Pa., leaves Tuesday, Thursday and Saturday at 7 A. M., and arrives at Philadelphia in 4 days by day light only, via Bridgewater, New Berlin, Mount Upton, North Bainbridge, South Bainbridge and Windsor to Mount Pleasant; where it intersects a line via Newburgh to New York, and also via Easton, Pa. to the city of Philadelphia.

Distance, from Utica to Mount Pleasant 116 miles. From Mount Pleasant to Philadelphia 140 miles. From Mount Pleasant to New York 110 miles. From Utica to Honesdale on the Delaware and Hudson canal 131 miles, and thence by railroad to Carbondale 15 miles.

Fare from Utica to Philadelphia $12.

☞ Expresses sent to any part of the country.

*Elisha Backus, Utica, G. T. Butler, Oswego, propri-
etors from Utica to Oswego.*

NORTHWARD.

Oswego mail, leaves daily, except the Sabbath, at
4 A. M. and arrives at Oswego same evening; via
Rome, Camden and Mexico. This line branches at
Williamstown, via Pulaski, Sacket's Harbor, and Adams to Watertown. At Pulaski it intersects a daily
from Watertown to Syracuse.

Distance, from Utica, to Pulaski 60 miles. From
Utica to Sacket's Harbor 90 miles. From Utica to
Watertown 94 miles. From Watertown to Syracuse
68 miles. From Utica to Oswego 76 miles.

*Elisha Backus, Utica, E. Merriam, Leyden, Buckley
& Symons, Watertown, proprietors.*

NORTHWARD.

Leaves daily at 4 A. M. and arrives at Sackets-Har-
bor same evening; via Trenton, (near Trenton Falls,)
Lowville and Watertown. This line branches at
Denmark three times a week to Ogdensburgh ; and at
Watertown 6 times a week via Cape Vincent to Og-
densburgh.

Distance, from Utica to Denmark 62 miles. From
Denmark to Ogdensburgh 64 miles. From Utica to
Watertown 81 miles. From Watertown to Ogdensburgh 64 miles. From Watertown to Cape Vincent
25 miles. From Utica to Sackets-Harbor 94 miles.

PACKETS.

Utica and Schenectady.

Three daily lines ply between Utica and Schenectady. The first line leaves Utica at 7½ A. M. The
second at 2 P. M. The third at 7 P. M. except the
Sabbath, when only the morning and evening boats
are run. Distance, 80 miles.

Utica, Rochester and Buffalo.

One daily line plies between these places, leaving
Utica at 1¼ P. M. Distance, from Utica to Rochester
160 miles. From Utica to Buffalo 253 miles.

Utica and Oswego.

One daily line plies between these places, leaving
Utica on the arrival of the last boat from Schenectady,
in the afternoon, say 5 o'clock. Distance, 101 miles.

Montezuma and Geneva.

Leaves Montezuma daily on the arrival of the packet from Utica, and arrives at Geneva from 5 to 6 P. M. Distance, 20 miles.

LIVERY STABLES.

Butterfield's, rear National Hotel and Chatfield's Inn.

Fellows', rear Baggs' Hotel, entrance from Main.

Lyman's, rear Union Hall, corner John and Main.

BOATS

Montezuma & Oneida Chief,

FOR the accommodation of passengers, on the Erie Canal, will perform their trips in future in the following order : Leave Utica and Montezuma every Monday, Wednesday and Friday morning at 8 o'clock, and meet at evening in Manlius ; proceed next day at 4 o'clock A. M. and arrive at Utica and Montezuma at 6 P. M.

Price of passage through the route including provisions and lodgings $4. Way passengers 3 cents per mile. Baggage at the owner's risk.

For passage apply at the Stage-Office in Utica, at the Inn of Richard Smith, Montezuma, or to the Captains on board.

July 1, 1820.—69 3m

N. B. Stages will be in waiting at most of the villages on the Canal, and at Montezuma, to convey passengers to the turnpike.

Old advertisements such as this, in the *Cayuga Republican,* September 6, 1820, demonstrate how the stagecoach complimented canal packet travel.

Chapter 9

The Canal and the Stagecoach

By 1821 the traveler could choose between the bumpy ride in the stagecoach over dusty turnpikes or the more leisurely pace of the packet boat.

The canal had been opened for navigation between Utica and Montezuma in May, 1820. This new mode of travel did not render the stagecoach obsolete as alluded to by some historians. It merely complimented it as subsidiary mode of travel. For the canal did not strike all of the communities across Upstate New York. Also, the stagecoach companies continued to hold the mail contracts which provided lucrative incomes.

If you were in a hurry or wanted to see more varied country, you might take the stage, rent an "extra" or provide your own conveyance. If travel was particularly heavy and one coach could not contain all applicants additional stages would be pressed into service. Occasionally three or four of these "extras" followed the regular coach.

By paying a price, usually the fare of seven passengers, an affluent traveler might reserve an "exclusive extra" for himself, family and servants in which none but his party and invited guests might enter. Such a charter was usually fitted out at his orders in regard to hours of arrival and departure, providing, however, the end of the journey terminated at the agreed time.

Canal packets at first were popular novelties. However, very few with the exception of emigrants went the entire distance of the waterway. Although the packet boat afforded an opportunity to "look around," the stagecoach offered variety and swiftness. Also the canal was frozen from four to five months of the year during which the stagecoach was unrivaled. At other seasons there was enough business for both packet and stage.

The canal was favored largely because it was less fatiguing, cheaper because meals and lodging were included in the fare, and one could get a good night's rest. Freight was the principal commodity of the canal. Frequenting packets were travelers, curious tourists or traveling families. Merchants, bankers and tradesmen bound to and from the metropolis, lawyers on their way to court and businessmen found the stage more convenient.

The stagecoach business was well established by the time the Erie Canal came into being. By 1821, stage routes covered the state, running through every major community on the map. For about two years Montezuma was the western terminus of the packets. Here, as at other places along the canal, stagecoaches met the packets to convey passengers to the main thoroughfares. Connections were so arranged to eliminate detention between packet and stage.

On August 3, 1821, the *Lyons Republican* noted the traveler could "choose between a continuation in post coaches, or take the Canal for 100 miles; by the latter mode he would behold that grand project, and form some idea of its vast advantages, but would forego the pleasures that the land conveyance always affords."

Serious construction problems in the Cayuga Marshes delayed the opening of that section of the canal until July 30, 1822. That day the packet "Myron Holley" passed through the newly-completed stretch from Lyons to Montezuma.

In August, William Faulkner of Geneva and W. W. Fenton of Montezuma established a daily line of stages connecting with the packets. The stage left Gooding's tavern in Canandaigua at 9 A.M. for Montezuma, also connecting with the steamboat "Enterprise" at Cayuga

Bridge. The returning stage conveyed passengers to Geneva and Canandaigua.

Evidence of the close association between stagecoach and packet is gleaned from old newspaper advertisements. In June, 1823, Samuel Allen established two daily north-south runs, between Palmyra and Canandaigua and Lyons and Geneva. The stages left Palmyra and Lyons respectively in the morning, returning in the afternoon to connect with packets; eastbound from Palmyra and westbound from Lyons.

An advocate of the canal noted canal packet passengers were charged only 4 cents a mile, including board and lodging, "both which are as good, if not better, than at the taverns on the road." He claimed the passage from Utica to Weed's Basin (Weedsport), 87 miles, was "as rapid as the stages travel, much less expensive, no risk of life or limb and no fatigue or dust attending."

The establishment of stage service between Geneva and Lyons in June, 1823, brought daily mail service to Lyons. In turn, the *Lyons Advertiser* was able to get out its weekly sheet on Wednesday instead of Friday. This coach left Woolsey's Tavern in Lyons at 5 A.M., returning from Geneva at 4 P.M. "Passengers on the canal whose business may require them to leave it for the Seneca Turnpike, will find the route a very pleasant one, and the carriages safe and expeditious." One proprietor assured that on this route passengers could be assured of punctuality and "sober and careful drivers will be furnished at all times."

Sources indicate a gradual improvement in stagecoach service in the early 1820s in conjunction with the canal. Stage lines radiated from such canal towns as Canajoharie, Utica, Chittenango, Syracuse, Weedsport, Montezuma, Lyons, Palmyra, Rochester and Lockport. At Buffalo there were excellent stagecoach accommodations in all directions with daily lines to Lewiston and Niagara Falls, as well as on the "Ridge Road" and the turnpike. The fare generally was four cents a mile.

Drawn with the Camera Lucida by Capt. B. Hall R.N.

Engraved by W. H. Lizars

Mile-long "Cayuga Bridge" across the north end of Cayuga Lake, was a miracle of construction in its day. It also was rendezvous point for steamboats and packets. — From "Forty Etchings, From Sketches Made with a Camera Lucida in North American in 1827 and 1828" by Capt. Basil Hall, R.N., 1828. *(Courtesy, Onondaga Historical Association)*

Competition was keen. In January, 1823, the "Old Line" syndicate of proprietors reduced stage fares to two cents a mile. W. W. Fenlon, now headquartered in Palmyra, established a line of stages in January, 1823, between Rochester and Auburn, via Palmyra, Lyons and Montezuma This appears to have been the first line of stages across Wayne County, east and west, and it operated over the newly-completed Montezuma Turnpike.

The stage was to leave Rochester at 3 A.M. Monday, Wednesday and Friday at 3 A.M., arriving in Auburn at 6 P.M. It left Auburn at 8 A.M. Tuesday, Thursday and Saturday, arriving in Rochester at 6 P.M. By this route, 10 miles would be saved. The taverns on this route at which the stages stopped "are not to be surpassed by any on the South Road. They are further informed, that not withstanding the great competition between the Old Line and the Opposition, and the low prices for which they carry passengers, travelers are assured they will find their expenses equally low by this line. Their horses and carriages will be at least as good as those of any other line."

The Erie Canal was opened with a grand celebration on October 26, 1825. It wasn't long before the benefits of this new waterway could be seen. At strategic points along the canal, stagecoaches and runners lined the docks to convey passengers to their destinations.

Montezuma tavern-keeper William H. Van Velzer ran a daily stage between his stand near the canal, to Cayuga, where it connected with the steamboat "Enterprise." It left Montezuma at 3 A.M. and returned "in time for passengers to catch the eastern packet boat." In 1824 there were two daily lines of westbound packets leaving Utica, making the 160 miles and 25 locks to Buffalo in 46 hours.

The impact of the Erie Canal on an upstate community is dramatized in an article from the *Rochester Album* and reprinted in the *Wayne Sentinel* published in Palmyra, on May 19, 1826.

"Since the completion of the canal, the travel

through this country has gradually though rapidly increased. There are now nine Lines of Stages that leave our Village (Rochester) daily and one semi-weekly, in the following manner: — Three via Canandaigua to Albany, one via Palmyra and Montezuma to Albany, one to Geneseo, one to Lewiston, one to Batavia Churchville, one to Penfield, all daily and one to Oswego, semi-weekly; besides which there is a departure of three Packet Boats daily, one east and two west. In addition to which, the transportation boats take a great share of passengers. At a modern calculation there depart daily the round number of 130 persons from this Village, the site of which only fourteen years ago (1812) was literally a forest. Within the limits of the corporation, we can enumerate rising 6,000 inhabitants, who for enterprise, are not a whit behind the Trojans of the North River. Rent continues high in consequence of the great demand for tenaments. If the country adjacent continues to improve as fast as it has done for ten years past, by the year 1835, Rochester will have outstripped Albany. Land in the vicinity is comparatively cheap and such farmers as have money and may wish to purchase land that will eventually be valuable cannot probably ever buy on better terms than at present."

In de Veaux's amusing and interesting guide to Saratoga Springs, Niagara Falls and Canada (published in Buffalo in 1841) he gives some interesting suggestions to prospective travelers which throw light upon the difficulties of travel. It serves as a good comparison between packet and stage travel.

Packet Boats

Enter your names as soon as you get on board, that you may have a berth, if you should remain over night. Do not put your head out of the cabin windows; keep below as much as practicable, and when on deck look ahead for the bridges, and before passing them come down on the lower afterdeck. For the feeble, and those who are worn with fatigue, the canal-boat offers the best accommodations. It glides along so quietly that you can repose and slumber as undisturbedly as in your own chamber.

Stage Coaches

"Of these old-fashioned conveyances little need be said. Ladies are always accommodated with the back seat. The middle seat is the easiest, the front seat the best to sleep on; but if you are subject to sickness when riding, always avoid it. Post coaches, if not crowded with too many passengers, over good roads, in fair weather, afford the most safe and agreeable mode of transit of any other; but the flyaway character of travelers is fast driving them out of use. From these vehicles the scenery of the country can always be advantageously viewed; and as the wheels roll on, the hours pass in social chat, free remark, amusing anecdotes and gay sallies, often truly pleasant and interesting."

Chapter 10

"The Nation's Guest"

Few individuals in American history have been accorded the public welcome as that received in 1824 and 1825 by General Lafayette. Although he had not been on American soil in nearly 40 years, Americans still looked upon him as the hero of the Revolution.

In 1777, at the age of 20, Lafayette came to America to aid in its cause, and his distinguished military accomplishments lifted the Revolution into the social register. In America his reputation has stood among the highest of generals and his generous and patriotic ardor in behalf of the cause of the colonies has been recognized by many leading American writers and speakers.

Now, at 67, thoroughly disenchanted by the French revolution and the Napoleonic madness that followed, Lafayette returned to the land of his dreams and greatest triumph. He came to America on the invitation of Congress and President James Monroe.

And no Roman returning from the wars was ever accorded a greater welcome. Lafayette then was the last surviving officer who served under General George Washington. The vast majority of people then living in the United States had been born since the Revolution. They transformed Lafayette into an idealized portrait of ancestral Revolutionary virtue; a living hero.

Lafayette arrived in New York City August 15, 1824, as cannon spread the news. A committee of 200 in six steamboats escorted him across the bay the next day as the West Point Military Academy band blared out "See the Conquering Hero Comes."

General Lafayette in 1825, although over 60, still retained his
youthful appearance of earlier times.

It is recorded that 50,000 of New York's 130,000 inhabitants jammed the Battery to greet him. Shops closed. Cannon boomed. Flags flapped. Loaded into a barouche drawn after Washington's preference by four white horses, and escorted by the committee, military officers and the Militia, and the Society of the Cincinnati.

Lafayette proceeded up Broadway to City Hall. The windows, balconies and roofs were filled with ladies waving handkerchiefs, in the days before ticker tape. New York pumped Lafayette's hand four days. It was an era of good feeling.

Then began the touring. It took five days and nights to reach Boston, so tumultuous was the greeting along the way. Farmers ran from the fields, children stood for hours by the roadside decked with ribbons on which the likeness of Lafayette was printed.

His road was arched with banners. So the typical pattern of his tour over the 24 states was now established. The Lafayette party traveled regularly till nearly midnight and was on the road again before dawn. The long line of coaches was always escorted from town to town by horsemen armed with torches.

Fires were kindled on the hills to warn of his approach, around which families would gather; kept awake by their anticipation of seeing the great Lafayette. Trumpets, bells, and cannon accompanied him everywhere.

Nearing a town, he would be greeted by a cloud of dust, out of which would emerge a horseback party of leading citizens—the mayor, judges, councilmen, maybe even a governor. After extended salutations, the Lafayette party would be escorted into the main street, to a specially fabricated stage, or to the leading hotel. On the balconies, the ladies gathered. Bells would ring and cannon fire would jar the glasses around the punch bowl.

Then there were the speeches. Every orator had a Lafayette speech polished for the occasion. Before Lafayette was allowed to rest, the whole procession must stop for the long receptional speech.

Lafayette, the true gentleman that he was, would stand there in spite of the hunger and fatigue while some mayor or president of the town insisted on telling him in Ciceronian periods how gloriously happy they felt to receive the good, the great, the venerated Lafayette.

The locals would then bow and shout a long and happy life to the beloved hero. But they did not let him go until he alighted, or delivered, standing in his carriage, some complimentary acknowledgements.

Then the crowd would rush in from every quarter; one an old companion, another the son or grandson of an aide-de-camp, an officer or a landlord of the Marquis when in America, and aging veterans of the Revolution. The escort dismounted, had the distinguished honor to shake hands with the nation's guest.

Only then was Lafayette permitted to arrive at his resting place and catch a few hours of sleep. But there, inevitably, he would be greeted by the committee on arrangements from the next town along the route.

New York City prepared for him the most magnificent fete that probably was ever seen in America up to that time. At Castle Garden, in an amphitheater, 600 feet in circumference, 6,000 persons attended a ball where 80 sets of cotillions were on the floor at the same time.

In Philadelphia, 160,000 citizens caroused in a parade while a printing press on a wagon was used to strike off odes for the occasion.

In Washington, Congress received him and later voted him $200,000 and a tract of land. In Yorktown, Lafayette revisited the scenes of his greatest military triumph, the storming of one of Cornwallis' redoubts. In Monticello, he visited the aged Thomas Jefferson.

From there, he continued southward to Charleston, Savannah, across Georgia and Alabama, down to New Orleans and up the Mississippi to St. Louis, leaving a trail of gaudy receptions.

At Nashville, Lafayette was entertained by the venerable Andrew Jackson. The party then took passage on the chartered steamboat "Mechanic" for Louisville. About

150 miles below Louisville, the steamer struck a snag and sunk.

The General and all the passengers got safely to shore, but his carriage, baggage and papers, as well as those of the other passengers, were lost, with the exception of five trunks.

The steamer "Paragon," loaded with freight for New Orleans, passing down the river shortly after the accident, was hailed by her owner, who happened to be a passenger on the "Mechanic." The "Paragon" returned the passengers safely to Louisville.

Later, the General was conveyed to Frankfort, Lexington, Cincinnati, Pittsburgh, and thence to Erie, Pa. Later, his luggage was recovered and forwarded.

At 2 A.M., Saturday, June 4, 1825, Lafayette arrived at Fredonia. At sunrise, he was met by the Buffalo committee at Dunkirk, where he embarked under a 13-gun salute on the Steam Brig, Capt. Sherman. The ship arrived at Buffalo at 2 P.M. amidst another 13-gun salute, which was answered by one of the 24 guns from the artillery stationed on a hill.

A procession was formed and Lafayette and company were escorted to the Eagle Tavern. That afternoon, he offered greetings and shook hands in a pavilion erected in front of the tavern. Here, he also had an interview with the famous Indian Chiefs Red Jacket and Pollard, of whom he made inquiries, that evinced a vivid recollection of Revolutionary scenes.

The night was spent at the Red Eagle Tavern and early Sunday morning, June 5, the General left for Black Rock, where he breakfasted, and was received in the court yard. At 10 A.M., in company with the committee and several others, he embarked at the new steam boat wharf, on board the canal boat "Seneca Chief."

The boat was towed through the harbor in front of the village for more than a mile, by three elegantly decorated barges, to the entrance of the canal. Here, two handsome sets of horses were in readiness, one of which was immediately attached to the flag boat and the other to the

"Seneca Chief." The party proceeded toward Tonawanda, where, at noon, Lafayette was received by the committee of Niagara County. He dined at the Eagle Hotel at Niagara Falls and spent considerable time admiring this great wonder.

The party spent the night at Lewiston, a pleasant village a few miles below the falls. The following day at 5 A.M., Lafayette took a carriage to Fort Niagara, where he was received with a 24-gun salute. The visit to the fort was short, and the party traveled to Lockport.

After proper toasts, greetings and salutation, the Lafayette party went aboard the canal boat "Rochester" bound for the city of the same name. Accompanying him were his son, George Washington Lafayette, and his secretary, A. Levasseur.

Levasseur wrote: "Although navigation by steam is not practicable on the canal, its banks not being defended by masonry, still, as the horses and tow-path are excellent, we travelled rapidly and, I must add, very commodiously; for the canal-boat Rochester, in which we were, contained many more of the conveniences of life than one could expect to find in so small a compass."

The boat reached Rochester very early the next morning, June 7th. The welcome at Rochester was merely a repeat performance of what had been experienced in other cities. At 6 A.M. a flotilla of 12 boats, one with a band on board, met the approaching boat with Lafayette aboard.

When the General's approach was signaled, the boats were ranged in a line, so that each could receive his salutation and announce him welcome as he passed. Lafayette returned the salute, boat by boat.

As they passed the crowded bridges, he presented himself on deck, and was hailed. The whole country was thronged with spectators, even on the house tops. On a splendid stage, erected over the center of the arch of the aqueduct over the Genesee River, he was received by a delegation and sat through long-winded speeches.

A party was held at Christopher's Mansion House, where a fine repast was served, followed by the customary toasting of the times. At 4 P.M. the General left for Canandaigua, via carriage. The party left the canal to visit the Finger Lakes.

That evening, he took supper at Blossom's Hotel, where he was received in handsome style. The night of June 7-8 was spent at the home of John Greig at his mansion on North Main Street. This house was later moved to 91 Gibson Street. Greig was a leading businessman and politician in the area.

A story persists that Mrs. Greig, in her vivacious and original way, wished to do high honor to the noted guest, and caused his bed to be literally heaped with roses, over which the bedding was spread.

But the perfume was too much for the old gentleman. He could not sleep, and a servant was called to remake the bed and remove the offending flowers.

The question has frequently been asked, "Why did Lafayette leave the Erie Canal at Rochester and travel overland to Syracuse?" Since it had been reported that he would travel via the canal from Lockport to Albany, all the receptions in the town from Rochester to Syracuse had to prepare to receive him on short notice.

One statement has been made there was a break in the canal. However, in Syracuse, he re-boarded the same boat "Rochester" for the trip eastward, which explodes this theory.

History states that Lafayette was a close friend of Robert Morris, a financier of Philadelphia who aided the cause of the Revolution. James Rees, later of Geneva, N. Y., was a clerk to Morris, and consequently was acquainted with Lafayette.

Rees was so respected and trusted by Robert Morris that when he was in financial difficulties in 1797 and a council was to be held with the western Indians near Geneseo to clear his title to all of western New York, west of the Phelps & Gorham Purchase, he sent Rees to Geneseo in July.

Rees had been sent to join Thomas Morris, son of Robert, then living in Canandaigua, to conduct the affairs connected with the treaty, known as the "Big Tree Treaty," executed in September, 1797.

Subsequently, Rees settled in Geneva, remaining there to his death on March 24, 1851. There is documentary proof that Rees was a friend of Morris.

Concerning the Lafayette visit, Rees was the first signature on an invitation dated May 28, 1825, which read:

Geneva, Ontario County, State of New York

28th May, 1825

GENERAL LA FAYETTE,

Dear Sir—We have been appointed by the Inhabitants of this Village, a Committee, to invite you to pay them a visit while on your tour through this section of the country.

Our vicinity was the theatre of some very interesting operations during the Revolutionary war, in which you acted so distinguished a part, with a generosity and disinterestedness which are without parallel in the history of the world.

It will afford our neighbors, and ourselves, the highest gratification to have an opportunity of expressing to you in person, the very grateful sense we entertain of the public services rendered by you to our country and of the great esteem we bear for your private virtues.

Hoping that it will be agreeable to you to gratify our wishes, we subscribe ourselves with every sentiment of respect and esteem, Dear Sir, your humble servants."

The invitation was also signed by Samuel Colt, Henry Dwight, John Shethar, Joseph Fellows, William Tillman, George Goundry, William S. De Zeng, Richard M. Bayly, John Sweeney and Phineas Prouty. The invitation was sent to Buffalo by special messenger. But being aware of the celerity of General Lafayette's movements, two of the committee were deputed to meet him on his arrival at Rochester and deliver a duplicate copy of this letter to him.

Lafayette was met here at Ball's Tavern by the Geneva contingent, some 10 miles east of Canandaigua on present Routes 5 and 20; then the old Seneca Turnpike.

The mission was satisfactorily accomplished, and on the morning of June 7th, an express arrived, bringing the good news that the General had accepted the invitation and would be in Geneva the following morning.

The committee hastily made all of the appropriate arrangements so that the General might be received in a suitable manner. Information was at once sent by express to the neighboring towns, and the response was prompt and spontaneous.

At about 7 A.M. June 8th, Lafayette and suite left Canandaigua and proceeded on their way towards Geneva, on the old Seneca Turnpike. At Gideon Ball's Tavern, about nine miles east of Canandaigua, the party was met by the Geneva contingent. Here, carriages were in waiting to receive the party. Lafayette's carriage, provided by William S. DeZeng, was drawn by six beautiful gray horses.

The party proceeded to Geneva under cavalry escort. As soon as they were in sight of the village, a signal gun was fired; the procession soon became a parade of military and civilians. Two lines were formed through which the carriages passed to a stage erected on the public square (now Pulteney Park), in front of which was a platform. The rear of the stage had columns supporting arches tastefully adorned with wreaths and flowers.

One reason Lafayette may have accepted the invitation to Geneva was that Rees, Captain John Shethar, a Revolutionary War veteran, and Mr. M. Camus, met him upon his arrival in Rochester. Camus may have been a special friend of Lafayette. The previous March, he had established a private school in French language in Geneva. According to the *Geneva Palladium*, Camus presented a personal letter signed by Lafayette introducing him to the citizens of Geneva.

Camus accompanied Lafayette to Boston. He then returned to Geneva where he conducted his school for more than a year.

"The Nation's Guest" was received at an elaborate reception at the "Franklin House" in Geneva. *(Photo courtesy P. B. Oakley, Geneva)*

Following the welcome at the town square, Lafayette was escorted to the Franklin House, which had only been recently opened. Following a breakfast attended by 200 people, a reception was held in the parlor.

Lafayette's right hand became so swollen from excessive handshaking, he was obliged to use his left hand, and then only to the ladies. He left Geneva at about 1 P.M. Transportation from Ball's Tavern to Geneva had been provided by William S. DeZeng, a prominent local businessman and merchant.

DeZeng had lately procured the elegant barouche from New York City, and graciously loaned it to carry the General and his traveling companions. It was drawn by six elegant white (some state gray) horses covered with flowers. The General was very impressed with the comfort and elegance of the carriage.

Lafayette was dispatched from Geneva to meet the Auburn delegation in the same carriage. So impressed were they with its superiority, the General did not change his seat, but proceeded to Auburn. Following ceremonies there, he again took his place in the same carriage and it was driven to Onondaga Hill.

There, the Syracuse committee, ashamed of their means of conveyance, kept the carriage for their own use. The General was thusly transported into the then village of Syracuse.

DeZeng, meanwhile, became concerned for the vehicle's safety and was obliged to send for it. It was returned, none the worse for wear by its passage over rough roads.

"It is now about two o'clock. The road of cannon, the music, the display of colors, the military, announce the welcome arrival of GENERAL LA FAYETTE." So wrote the editor of the *Waterloo Gazette* on June 8, 1825.

Here, Lafayette was entertained at the Waterloo House. But the otherwise joyous occasion was marred earlier in the day when a man was killed attempting to fire a cannon. It was a holiday and the streets were thronged with people. A small cannon placed in the square had been fired at intervals.

Not content with an ordinary load, a double charge of powder was put in and a mass of flax rammed in upon it, the charge being still further compressed by driving upon the rammer with an axe. An unsuccessful attempt was made to fire it.

Captain Jehiel P. Parsons happened by, and unaware of the manner in which the piece was loaded, touched it off. The cannon blew up and Parsons was killed instantly; being literally blown in two just above the hips.

General Lafayette was not made aware of this incident until he was well beyond Waterloo. It is said he expressed much regret over the circumstances and would have returned to console the family if time had permitted. He sent back a deputation to inquire of the particulars of the accident and the circumstances of the bereaved family. Captain Parsons left a mother, three sisters and a brother who depended on him for support. Apparently, feeling somewhat responsible for the Captain's death, Lafayette later sent his mother a draft for $1,000, accompanied by the following letter:

Philadelphia, Pa., July 26, 1825

Dear Madam:

The dreadful event, which took place on the morning of my introduction to the citizens of your town, when it became known to me, filled my heart with the most painful and sympathetic emotions. Every subsequent information relative to the melancholy loss of your son, could not but inhance those feelings.

Permit me to avail myself of our community of regrets, to obtain from you and assent to the offer which may not afford to you, but will to me some consoling relief. Learning the situation of the family, the acceptance of the enclosed bill of One Thousand Dollars, will confer upon me a great obligation. Be pleased, dear madam, to receive my affectionate and condoling respects.

La Fayette.

In Auburn, Lafayette was entertained at the "Western Exchange" on
Genesee Street, present site of W. T. Grant Co. department store.

From Waterloo, Lafayette proceeded to Cayuga
Bridge, where he arrived at 4 P.M. Here, he was met by
the Auburn delegation. The party halted here a few moments to partake of refreshments while the horses were
changed. Lafayette then reseated himself in DeZeng's
barouche. The six elegant chestnut horses were furnished
unsolicited by Isaac and John M. Sherwood. Also seated
in the carriage was Judge Throop of Auburn.

The scene of Auburn was much a repeat performance
of the other communities; a parade and a grand reception at the leading hotel.

There were speeches, much handshaking and embrac-
ing of aging Revolutionary War veterans. Dinner was
served on the lawn at the rear of the Western Exchange—
then called Hudson's Hotel. This was followed by a Ball.

Lafayette left Auburn at 11 P.M. and entered Skaneateles at 1 A.M. on the morning of June 9th. "We had a
grand time when Lafayette passed through this village,"
wrote Samuel Addison Porter on June 25, 1825, in a
letter. "We had erected a Splendid Arch on the East End

of the Bridge, decorated with Flowers and Flags and appropriate design and inscription. The whole bridge was lined with trees brought from the woods. He passed here about One o'clock at night.

"The whole village was illuminated, and not the least was the appearance of our house among the rest. The arch over the bridge was lighted and lamps were interspersed among the trees the whole length of the bridge. We had also the barrels on fire scattered along in front of Hall's Hotel where he stopped and was presented to a great number of the ladies and gentlemen of the village. Capt. Morse anchored his Seventy Four off the bridge and fired One Gun on his arrival. The Auburn Escort were delighted with the appearance of the village as they came over the Hill and Slover's Old House. On the whole I think Skaneateles did itself Honor for once and likewise the Marquis."

The party was soon on its way to Marcellus. When the little cavalcade was discovered by their lamps descending the hill into the main street, the bells announced the fact. The village was similarly lighted and people had waited up all night in anticipation of the General's arrical.

After appropriate toasts at Beach's Hotel, the entourage was soon on the way to Onondaga Hill, over the old Seneca Turnpike. They arrived at 4:30 A.M. and after an exchange of congenialities, proceeded to Onondaga Hollow.

A heart-warming experience occurred here, which was published in the *Onondaga Register* of June 15th.

"A very affecting scene took place while Gen. La-Fayette was passing through this village, on Thursday last, in the recognition by him of one of his former companions in arms, by the name of Ebenezer Moore. On being informed that one of the soldiers of the revolution was near him, the General ordered the carriage to stop and manifested a wish to see him. Moore was immediately introduced, and on approaching once more the man under whom he fought, bled and suffered for his country, he was greatly affected, and with much difficulty succeeded in informing the General that his Captain's name was Olney, and that he and his Captain were the two first who ascended the British redoubt at the battle of Yorktown. The good Lafayette, grasping his hand with all the warmth of affectionate recognition, said, 'I am very glad to see that man once more this side of the grave . . . ' "

Much jubilation met Lafayette in Syracuse, where a reception was held at Williston's Hotel. Arriving there at 6 A.M., he was welcomed by the cheers of thousands and the roar of cannon. The General remained here until 9 A.M., when he boarded the Canal Packet Boat, "Rochester," to continue his trip to Boston.

In less than 24 hours, Lafayette had covered 75 miles, from Canandaigua to Syracuse; by traveling night and day. This was fast traveling and demanded much physical endurance. The weather was hot.

But every effort was made by the communities through which he passed to facilitate his progress. His private secretary, Levasseur, commented: " . . . we were struck with the excellence of the horses which formed our relays; and we were afterwards informed that they had been furnished by citizens, whose patriotic disinterestedness was highly appreciated by the different committees appointed to conduct the General."

Notwithstanding all that was done to lessen the hardships of the overland journey, the travelers were glad to reach the canal again at Syracuse. Levasseur wrote: "We resumed our journey with more pleasure, because we had suffered much with heat and dust in our last day's ride. The General formed the design of travelling day and night while on the canal, and stopping at the towns he should meet with on the voyage, only long enough to express his gratitude to the inhabitants, all of whom had made preparations for his arrival."

Thus ended General Lafayette's arduous, but long-remembered journey over the stage roads of Central New York in 1825.

In their younger days, every tavern had its "champion dogs."

Interlude

Sour Old Dogs

(From the *Auburn Bulletin,* July 2, 1870)

The race is almost extinct — relic of old stage times, when every tavern (stage-house) had its champion dog, the pet of the table, the pride of the hostlers and drivers, and the terror of good little boys and egg thieves — useful dogs with teeth.

But the stages have disappeared. The glory of those taverns has departed. The dog still lingers here and there. We have seen one now and then at Ithaca, Geneva, Cazenovia and other old stage towns.

The venerable survivors own the bar-rooms, but they say nothing. They are fat — too fat to scratch themselves. So they rub and rub, and rub their hair off in silent discontent. Two trips a day they make to the barn and superintend it. They are older than the man who attends to the livery. They eye him with red, unhappy eyes.

They lift their flabby lip to show where teeth once were. Useless old dogs! They have seen changes. They belong to the house. They are the oldest inhabitants — theirs is a vester right. Let no cheerful stranger chirp to them, their youth and vanity is gone.

Let no child pat them; they attend to their own itch cure. Let the poor old beast sleep out his days at home and never mind his sour growl at whatever new or cheerful things arrests his attention. — He will not last long.

He cannot bite. He never plays. He only growls and keeps his place. By and by he will die, and his care-taking, yet discontented spirit, shall slowly wander hither and

thither superintending affairs until he finds some dwell-
ing place congenial — some man of kindred soul, then
let him enter and dwell — and taking turns let them bless
the world with harmless, helpless, toothless, useless fault-
finding.

— T. K. Beecher.

*   *   *   *   *

OBSERVATIONS OF STAGECOACH TRAVEL
IN 1838

Excerpts from Vol. 11, *America, Historical, Statistic,
and Descriptive* by J. S. Buckingham, New York, 1841)

On the morning of Wednesday, August 8, we left
Utica in an extra, as the regular stage had set out in the
middle of the night, and proceeded on by the high turnpike road towards Syracuse, where we intended making
our next halt. It is not usual to travel in postchaises in
this country, but, in lieu of this, extra coaches, with nine
seats will be furnished on any part of the road, if the persons engaging them will pay the regular stage-fare for
eight passengers. We were fortunate in finding an agreeable party of three persons, which, added to our own of
the same number, enabled us to take an extra between
us and divide the expense; and in this way the carriage
is entirely under the direction of the party occupying it
as to stoppages, hours of setting out, etc.

These coaches, whether stage or extra, are very heavily built, though airy and commodious when the passengers are once seated. The baggage is all carried in a large
leather case projecting from behind, and the coaches are
painted with very gaudy colors.

The horses are large, strong, and good; but the harness
is coarse, ill-fitted, and dirty. There is no guard and no
outside passenger; and the coachman, or driver, as he is
here universally called, is generally very ill-dressed,
though civil, and well qualified for his duty, notwithstanding that he receives no fees whatever from any of
the passengers by the way; and it is certainly an agree-

able thing for an English traveller to find himself on the road, with his fare paid once for all, without the frequent opening of the coach door for the shilling and half crown due, by usage, to the coachman or guard, with a certainty of insolent language if it be not readily paid.

The rate of stage-travelling varies between six and eight miles the hour, but is more frequently the former than the latter. The roads are in general wretched, full of deep ruts and elevations, that jolt and shake the traveller to a painful degree; while, in appearance, the American stagecoach, with its horses, harness, and fittings, is as inferior to the light, smart, and trim coaches of Bath, Brighton, and Dover, that start from Charing Cross and Piccadilly, as a heavily-laden merchant-like ship is to a beautiful corvette or light frigate, or — to do the Americans justice in another department, in which they excel us — as the deeply-laden collier going up the Thames is to one of their beautiful pilot schooners or packets.

While on this subject, I may mention that a great many even of the coach-phrases in America are derived from a seafaring life; as, for instance, instead of the coachman coming to the door, as in England, and asking, "Are ye all in, gentlemen?" the American driver's question is, "Are ye all aboard?" and instead of the signal of the English guard, "All right," which precedes the crack of the whip, the American bookkeeper, when he hands up the waybill, exclaims, "Go ahead!" — pp. 126-127.

We found it most convenient, as our party consisted of four, to take an "exclusive extra," as a private hired carriage is called, to convey ourselves and all our baggage, which gave us the entire command of our own time in setting out and arriving; and as these "extras" are always of the full size of stage-coaches, with seats for nine inside, we rode at great ease. Yet, though we had this roomy vehicle and four good horses, which, with the driver, was changed every eight or ten miles, the expense was less than a postchaise would have cost in England. —p. 187.

Chapter 11

Southern Tier Stagecoach Days

The frontier outpost of Owego was the hub of the stagecoach business serving the southern tier and northern Pennsylvania.

The first regular stage to visit Owego came from Newburgh; it being a three-horse lumber wagon owned by Samuel Stanton, a tavern-keeper in Mount Pleasant, Pa. Stanton was instrumental in the opening of this western route.

The road ran west from Newburgh, via Monticello to the Delaware River. It then cut across northeastern Pennsylvania to Great Bend, on the Susquehanna, and on through Binghamton to Owego, Ithaca and Geneva.

This series of roads contributed greatly to the early prosperity of Newburgh, and for many years, herds of cattle, sheep, etc., and wagons of grain and produce flowed in a steady stream to the Hudson.

The route was over the Newburgh and Cohecton Turnpike, and from there to Great Bend over the Cohecton and Great Bend Turnpike. This route was completed in 1811. The road was free of toll to Owego.

The Owego and Ithaca Turnpike was laid out and partially improved in 1808, and the Ithaca and Geneva Turnpike, via Trumansburg, was constructed in 1811.

In 1810, Conrad Teeter contracted to carry the mail once a week from Sunbury, Pa., to Painted Post via Athens, Pa., then called Tioga Point. His vehicle was a one-horse wagon. Teeter succeeded a mail carrier who had been delivering the mails in a pouch on horseback.

Conrad Teeter's early "stagecoach" probably looked something like this.

Teeter's enterprise was successful and he soon was delivering the mail in a covered wagon pulled by two horses. For a few years he carried the mails between Painted Post and Wilkes Barre, Pa., making the round trip once a week. After a time, he ran a covered Jersey carriage, drawn by four horses, between Wilkes Barre and Athens.

Teeter was one of the more interesting characters of early staging in the Susquehanna region. He weighed over 300 pounds and was of a jovial disposition. He always pointed out "my" farms to the passengers, usually claiming the finest along the way.

When asked why he drove stage, he replied he lived to rein four horses and drive, but had "no taste for farming." Teeter was famed for his knowledge of people and places, and his fund of good yarns.

He went to Owego in 1811 and succeeded Mr. Stanton as proprietor of the Newburgh and Owego route. He drove the stage himself, making weekly trips. FromNewburgh, passengers went by water to New York. This stage went over the route later taken in by the famed Newburgh and Geneva line of Oliver Phelps.

At this time, Mr. Teeter had a partner named Huntington. Teeter's brother-in-law, Miller Horton of Wilkes
Barre, had taken over the mail route between there and
Athens. He came to Owego and became Teeter's partner
after the partnership with Huntington was dissolved.

Oliver Phelps of Ludlowville, a successful businessman and merchant in the Ithaca area, joined Teeter's
business in 1816. On February 14th of that year, Teeter
and Phelps were granted a legislative monopoly between
Newburgh and Geneva, and Ithaca and Auburn.

The "exclusive right" was for a term of six years, and
violators were subject to a fine of $500. The law enacted
by the State Legislature prescribed that trips be made in
three days, twice a week; more frequent if the public demanded it. The fare was not to exceed seven cents a mile.

.This Oliver Phelps (1779-1809) should not be confused with Oliver Phelps (1749-1809), the merchant and
land speculator of Ontario County.

In 1816, a new company was formed with Oliver
Phelps at its head, and Ithaca was made western termi-
nous of the route instead of Owego. An improved line of
stages was established with tri-weekly trips through to
Ithaca and Geneva and Auburn.

Phelps was responsible for construction of the first
commercial steamboat on Cayuga Lake, the "Enterprise of Ithaca." The vessel made its maiden voyage to
Cayuga and return on June 7, 1820, inaugurating a new
era of transportation in the Finger Lakes Region.

One June 7, 1820, the *Ithaca Journal* stated:

> "The Enterprise is connected with a line of stages
> from Newburgh to Buffalo, and thus furnishes to tra-
> vellers from New York, and others going west, one of
> the most expeditious and pleasant routes through the
> State. The stage runs from Newburgh to this village
> in two days; thus travellers may leave New York at
> 5 P.M., in a steamboat, the second day arrive in Ith-
> aca, go aboard the steamboat Enterprise the same
> night; receive good accommodations, and rest in

Rapid Travelling.

THE NEWBURGH & GENEVA LINE OF
STAGES,

DURING the summer and fall months, will leave Newburgh on Mondays, Wednesdays and Fridays, immediately on the arrival of the Steam-Boats from New-York, and running through Montgomery, Bloomingburgh, Monticello, Cochecton, Mount-Pleasant, Great-Bend, Binghamton and Owego, will arrive at Ithaca in TWO DAYS; and from thence to Geneva the next morning. Returning, will leave Ithaca the same days, (the stage from Geneva having arrived the evening previous,) and arrive in Newburgh the second day, in season to take the Steam-Boat to New-York.

By the above arrangement, it will be seen that the whole route from New-York to Geneva will be performed in little more than two days and a half, affording a facility of communication and accommodation to men of business superior to any Line in the state. The rich variety of country, and the pleasant villages through which the stage passes, together with the very moderate rates of *fare*, and cheapness of living on the road, all conspire to invite the traveller and man of business to patronise this line.

At Geneva this line intersects several lines of daily stages, which run from thence to Canandaigua, Buffalo, Rochester, Lewiston, and the Falls of Niagara, as well as other places of notoriety bordering on the Grand Canal.

No pains will be spared to render the accommodations of passengers safe and pleasant; and they may rest assured that they will find good horses and carriages, sober, attentive drivers, and good houses of entertainment.

☞ SEATS in the above Line may be taken at Faulkner's Hotel, Geneva; C. De Mott's Hotel, Ovid; Spencer's Hotel, Ithaca; Union Coffee-House, Owego; Robinson's Hotel, Binghamton; I. Mott's, New-Milford; E. C. St. John's, Mount-Pleasant; Baird's and Godfrey's Hotels, Bloomingburg; Crawford's and French's Hotels, Newburgh; and at most of the public houses on the route.

O. PHELPS,
and others, Proprietors.

May 20, 1824.   n'55tf

Oliver Phelps was the "Sherwood" of the stage business in the southern tier as evidenced by this old advertisement.

comfortable 'births' during the passage; resume the stage next morning at Cayuga Bridge, and the same night arrive in Buffalo; making the whole route in three days — one day sooner than is performed by way of Albany."

The fare on the "Enterprise" was $1.00 each way. Later, Phelps sold the vessel to Captain Elijah H. Goodwin for $2,000, and it was dismantled about 1831.

One of Phelps' inventions was the "American Watercoach," a horse boat that plied the Seneca River between Cayuga Bridge and Montezuma. The *American Journal* of Ithaca, July 3, 1822, described the vehicle as "an ingenious horseboat. This boat is a pleasing change from the monotonous movement of canal boats to the more animated motion of the 'American Watercoach' as the proprietor has happily named it. The conveyance in this boat is pleasing and safe. It is handsomely fitted for the accommodation of 20 or 30 passengers."

This vessel, which connected with the stage lines, operated on a horse treadmill arrangement. Phelps filed a patent for an "elastic floor for propelling boats" on November 17, 1821. How long this boat was in operation is not known, but presumably it was in operation at least until the Erie Canal was completed across the Montezuma Marshes in October, 1822.

A statement of mail contracts in 1821 prepared by the U.S. Postmaster General shows that Oliver Phelps & Co. received $7,000 that year for transporting the mail from Newburgh to Geneva. Proprietors such as Phelps, unable to do all the work themselves, sub-let these contracts to local operators.

Apparently, some of these operators incurred debts and, fearing he might be held liable for them, Mr. Phelps published the following statement in the *Ithaca Journal* on January 8, 1823:

"Know all Men,

That I, Oliver Phelps, have been employed by the Postmaster General to carry the United States

Three times a Week

From Geneva to Penn-Yan.

Leaves Geneva Mondays, Thursdays & Saturdays.
Leaves Penn-Yan Tuesdays, Fridays & Sundays.

MAIL STAGES have commenced and will run regularly twice a week from Owego, by the way of Tioga Point, Chemung, Elmira, Big Flats, Painted Post, Campbelltown, Bath, Howard, Hornellsville, Dansville, Geneseo and Avon, to Rochester. Also, to Olean Point by way of Bath and Angelica—through in less than 3 days—*Fare*, $6 25. Leaves Owego and Rochester Wednesdays and Sundays.— From Geneva by Penn-Yan, Wayne, Bath, Howard, Hornellsville, Almond, Angelica, Friendship, Oil Creek, to Olean Point— through in 2 1-2 days—*Fare*, $5 00. Leaves Geneva Mondays and Thursdays; Olean, Wednesdays and Sundays.

These lines meet regularly at Bath and Hornellsville, so that travellers may pass to either section without delay. They intersect, at Geneva and Avon, the Albany and Buffalo lines; at Rochester, the Lewiston line; at Geneseo, the Canandaigua & Moscow line; at Painted Post, a line to Williamsport, Pa.; at Elmira, a line to the latter place—also, a line from Berwick, Pa. to Geneva, by way of Ovid; at Tioga Point, a line to Wilkesbarre; at Owego, the several lines from N. York, Milford, Newburgh and Ithaca, Washington City, Baltimore, Philadelphia, Lancaster, Easton, Harrisburgh, Northumberland, Wilkesbarre, Montrose, &c.

Good Horses, new Coaches, and careful, attentive Drivers are employed. Every attention will be paid to the comfort and safety of Passengers. The Proprietors have expended large sums in establishing these lines, and are determined to conduct them at all times in such manner as to merit a liberal patronage.   JOHN MAGEE, of Bath, and Others, PROPRIETORS.

January 1, 1825.

N. B.—Boats and Skiffs of all sizes will be constantly kept at Olean to accommodate such as may wish to descend the Allegany river, during the months of April, May, June, July, October, November and the fore part of December. Travellers may generally pass from Geneva to Pittsburgh in about 5 or 6 days. When there are two or more in company, their whole expenses will not exceed ten dollars each.

John Magee of Bath pretty much monopolized the stagecoach business in southwestern New York State. This is one of his old advertisements.

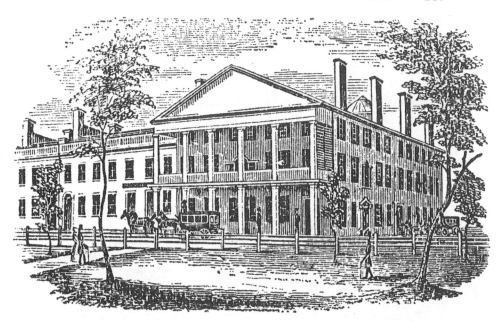

Geneva Hotel was the earliest terminus for stage lines from all directions in the early decades of the 19th century. It also was famous for its "hanging gardens" on the hillside facing Seneca Lake. It is now an apartment complex. (*Courtesy, Geneva Historical Society*)

mail for five or six years past, on the routes from Newburgh to Geneva, and from Ithaca to Auburn. Not being able to perform all this labour myself, I have employed others to carry said mail, at their own expense — some of whom I have given all that I received, and some I have given but a part, and furnished them with horses or carriages. The whole of the routes have been put out in the above ways, for two years past. A number of different persons have been employed, during that period, especially on that part of the route between Owego and Newburg. And having lately made some new arrangements, and contracted with some other persons, on the route from Chenango to Ithaca, and from Ithaca to Geneva, and Auburn, at which time and since, some of the good people of Ithaca have urged, that it was the duty of the original contractors for carrying the mail, to give public notice that they did not consider themselves holden to pay other carriers' debts — although it may be disagreeable to post every person that makes a contract with me, yet if it is necessary, they will pardon me if I do so. And I do therefore hereby post, and publicly declare, that I will not pay any debts hereafter made or contracted by the person who has contracted to carry the mail, between Chenango and Owego; and I also post, and publicly declare, that I will not pay any debts hereafter contracted by the person who has engaged to carry the mail, between Owego and Ithaca, and I also post all others, with whom I have contracted.

I likewise expect to agree with some good faithful person, at the opening of the spring, to run carriages from Ithaca village to the Steam-boat, during the running of said boat next season, and intend to furnish them with some horses and carriages, to enable them to accommodate the public and give them all they can make besides: and I expect to contract with some one or more persons, to cart, from the Lake to Owego,

When launched in 1820 through the efforts of Oliver Phelps, the "Enterprise" was the first commercial steamboat on Cayuga Lake. *(Courtesy DeWitt Historical Society of Tompkins County)*

next season, Two HUNDRED TONS OF PLASTER, for which I will give the HIGHEST PRICE, and the use of a couple of old horses in the bargain — but, I must inform them, that they also stand posted, as I am determined not to pay debts contracted by any other person except myself. And although the Postmaster General neglected to advertise me, when he employed me to carry the United States mail, I hope the good people of Ithaca will not present any demands they may have against me, to him for payment.

January 7, 1823."

Mr. Phelps moved to St. Catharines, Ontario, Canada, in September, 1824, where he entered into a contract with others to build 34 wooden locks on the Welland Canal. Subsequently, he sold his property in Ludlowville and withdrew from the stagecoach business. The line of stages to Auburn and some property were sold to Isaac Sherwood.

In later years, the Phelps routes and others were operated by Jesse and Chauncey L. Grant, father and son and proprietors of Grant's Coffee House in Ithaca. In the 1830's they had an interest in the three existing lines to the Hudson River, as well as those west and northwest from Ithaca to Elmira, Bath, Auburn and Geneva.

Evidence shows that in the latter half of the stagecoach era the proprietors on all three of these routes combined together under working agreements, similar to the "Old Line" to the north.

Individual proprietors put in as many coaches and horses as were needed to operate the number of miles each was responsible for, and drew out of the common treasury receipts in proportion to their mileage. Once every three months meetings of the proprietors were held to balance the books, settle the accounts and set policy.

To trace the history of the many stage lines in the southern tier is not within the scope of this work, which is primarily concerned with the "Old Line Mail" and its proprietors. However, a brief chronology may be in order:

One of the most impressive inns on the stage line from Ithaca to Auburn was the "Rogues Harbor Inn" at Libertyville (now South Lansing). Even today, it is a popular eating place.

1816—Stephen B. Leonard established first line from Owego to Bath; became daily service in 1819.

1814-1820—Service established westward to Angelica, Olean.

January, 1824—Group of proprietors establish line in competition with the Newburgh route, via Milford and Montrose, Pa.

May, 1827—Bath to Canandaigua service established, via Cohocton, Naples and Rushville, intersecting line to Dansville and Prattsburgh.

September, 1828—Tri-weekly service established from Owego to Seneca Lake, connecting with steamboat "Seneca Chief" at Watkins Glen.

April, 1830—New daily line, Owego to Rochester, via Tioga Point, Elmira, Painted Post, Bath, Cohocton, Dansville, Geneseo and Avon, "through in two days." "T. J. Magee & Others, Proprietors."

October, 1840—N. Randall & Co., opposition line, Owego
to Morristown, New Jersey, via Montrose, Carbondale, Honesdale and Milford. Unsuccessful
and driven from the road. Sold out.

October, 1843—"Eagle Line" of Field, Fox & Co. established after New York & Erie Railroad completed
to Middletown, to Owego, via old Newburgh
route.

When the Erie Railroad reached Owego on October
1, 1849, the days of the old stage lines were at an end so
far as this part of the state was concerned. The old
coaches disappeared, most of them being removed to parts
of the country yet untouched by railroads.

A typical rural country tavern on Phelps' far-flung system was the "Sherwood
House" at Sherwood. Building, still standing, was for many years a hospital,
and is now a private residence.

Chapter 12

The "Pioneer Line"

Strict observance of the Sabbath was a topic which stirred much controversy in the 1820s. From their lofty pulpits the clergy condemned the stagecoach and steamboat lines for operating on Sunday.

It was also the theme of discussion in the streets, at political debates and in the newspapers. Many espoused the cause while others questioned the wisdom of the course pursued by its advocates.

Taking advantage of the situation, a group of enterprising businessmen saw this as an opportune time to put a competing line of stages on the road to operate six days only and not on Sunday.

After holding several mass meetings to gain support from the church and the public, the "Pioneer Line" of stagecoaches was formed. One such meeting was held in Auburn on February 13, 1828, attended by 22 delegates; a few of whom were old competitors of the "Old Line" and the rest regarded as "men of extraordinary zeal in matters of religion."

Auburn's citizens were astonished to find that as a result of this body's deliberations, commissioners were appointed to establish a line of stages to run from Albany to Buffalo Monday through Saturday only. Those attending the convention pledged their "patronage, support, influence and exertion," declaring it to be in the "cause of the Lord Jesus Christ, and that it must prevail."

Subscriptions were circulated through the state and larger sums of money were raised for the new line. The

Rochester Observer of April 25, 1828, advertised the line would inaugurate service on June 2nd. The coaches would be "made light; being low, painted white, and trimmed with green. They will travel with great expedition, but never run horses with another line.

"The fare on these lines is not to exceed the present rate of other lines; but will not condescend to underbid other lines, or be continually varying their fare if underbid by them."

The "Old Line" proprietors agreed that a due observance of the Sabbath was in the best interest of society. "But we do not believe any people can be coerced to become moral or religious, nor do we agree with the convention, that 'travelling in stages on our Lord's day can be prevented' in the present state of public sentiment."

A fair opportunity for testing the experiment was made by the "Old Line." The Pioneer Line could buy them out, and they would withdraw from the business, at a "fair and reasonable price."

The "Pioneer" proprietors said the proposal was "fair at first view, but it comes too late. Contracts for new stages are already made, and an entire new establishment is demanded."

The following appeared in the *Onondaga Register*, April 16, 1828:

TO THE PUBLIC

A CIRCULAR, dated *Utica, January 31st, 1828*, signed by ABRAHAM VARICK, ELIZUR GOODRICH, EDWARD VERNON, SPENCER KELLOGG, A. M. BEEBE, THOMAS CHRISTIAN, AND WALTER KING, was published, recommending a Convention of Delegates from the towns and villages of the western districts of this state to assemble at Auburn on the 13th of February, to agree on measures for "establishing and supporting a line of stages from Albany and Troy to Buffalo and Niagara Falls," which shall not travel on the Sabbath.

A Convention was held pursuant to this notice, from which emanated an address and resolutions signed by

ELIHU EWERS, Chairman, SPENCER KELLOGG, Secretary, M. C. Reed; Edward Vernon, Jn. Sloan, jr. Perez Hastings, Ira Gould, Artemus Stone, Ephraim Scovill, Lyman Grandy, E. Dean, John Perrine, Amaziah How, Seth Hastings, jr., Richard Steel, Josiah Bissel, jr., Israel Huntington, Theodore Spencer, Edson Carr, Hiel Warner, William Brown, Henry Bradley, Delegates; "pledging their patronage and support to a line of stages between Albany and Buffalo, which shall not travel on the Sabbath." They also appointed John T. Norton of Albany, Jonathan Crane of Schenectady, Elizur Goodrich, Abraham Varick, and Edward Vernon of Utica, William Brown of Auburn, William Tillman of Geneva, Henry W. Taylor and Walter Hubbell of Canandaigua, Aristarchus Champion, William Atkinson, and Josiah Bissell, jr., of Rochester, and Thaddeus Joy of Buffalo, *Commissioners,* to establish the proposed line of stages.

The proprietors of several lines of stages running on the two great roads from Albany and Troy, to Buffalo and Niagara Falls, feeling themselves called upon to notice these proceedings. Some of us have been engaged in this business since the first establishment of public stages in this state. — We all of us became so engaged, expecting like honest men in other callings, to provide a living for ourselves and families, by the exertions of honest industry. We have not claimed, nor do we expect the patronage of the public beyond what is fairly due to those who faithfully serve them in this or any other capacity. We admit the truth of the maxim, that a fair competition is the life of business, and while the spirit of our laws and public sentiment adhere to this principle, so long do we believe they will be a guarantee of individual and national prosperity. We have often had competitors in our business, and expect them again; but we did not expect an *opposition,* (for opposition it will prove) emanating from a *Convention* called to promote a due observance of the *Sabbath.*

As individuals, we rejoice at every evidence of increasing religion and morality. They afford the best security for the permanence of our civil as well as our religious liberties, and we shall at all times feel it our happiness as well as our duty to concur in such reasonable measures as will best support the institutions of religion. We believe a due observance of the Sabbath essential to the best interest of society. In no ordinance is the wisdom of Omniscience more apparent than in the institution of the Holy Sabbath, and every effort calculated to promote its due observance, deserves the cordial cooperation not only of every Christian, but of every well wisher to society. But we do not believe any people can be coerced to become moral and religious, nor do we agree with the convention, that "travelling in stages on the Lord's day can be prevented" in the present state of public sentiment. Such efforts must follow, but cannot control public opinion. But while we commend the motives of the Convention, we have no disposition to oppose their efforts.

If they and their friends have confidence in the feasibility of this object, we will aid their views, by putting them in possession of our stage property for a fair equivalent, and withdraw from the business. It is most obvious that this will give the greatest possible facility for effecting the objects of the Convention. They will commence with the important aid of a well arranged and firmly established line of Stages, and avoid the formidable and well known evils which uniformly attend contending stage lines.

As a proof of our readiness to make good these assurances, we, the undersigned, now offer to sell to the Commissioners appointed by the convention, or their friends, our entire stock of Horses, Harness, Coaches, Carriages, Wagons, Sleighs, and other property immediately connected with the running of stages, which are now employed by us on the two great roads from Albany and Troy, to Buffalo and Niagara Falls, at a fair and reasonable price, to be estimated by three competent persons, to be agreed upon by the vendors and vendees, and to give liberal credit to the purchasers on approved security.

If this offer is not embraced by the Commissioners, we here inform the public that any person who shall lie by at the usual stopping places of the stages on Saturday evening, from conscientious design to observe the Sabbath, shall have the privilege of pursuing his journey the Monday following in our stages, without any additional charge for stage fare.

We are unwilling to close this address, without acknowledging our obligations to the public, and to our friends, for the encouraging support they have from time to time afforded us. And while we continue in this employment, no exertions shall be spared by us to deserve their continued confidence and support.

JASON PARKER,
A. SHEPARD,   *Utica,*
S. D. CHILDS,
T . S. FAXTON,
ISAAC SHERWOOD, *Skaneateles,*
J. M. SHERWOOD, *Auburn*
C. H. COE, & CO., *Canandaigua,*
ADAMS & BLINN, *Rochester,*
B. & S. BARTON, *Lewiston,*
B. D. COE, *Buffalo,*
E. PHILLIPS, *Syracuse,*
S. GOODWIN, *Madison,*
Wm. STOREY, *Cherry Valley,*
ASA SPRAGUE, *Schenectady,*
A. THORP, *Albany,*

Utica, April 1, 1828

Thus their offer was rejected and the gauntlet thrown down for the stagecoach war which ensued.

The journals of the day were in sympathy with the "Old Line" and felt the offer to sell out their interests gave the "Pioneer" a good opportunity to "take over." The "Old Line" proprietors promised their patrons:

"If this offer is not embraced by the Commissioners, we here inform the public that any person who shall lie at the usual stopping places of the stages on Saturday evening, from the conscientious design to observe the Sabbath, shall have the privilege of pursuing his journey the Monday following in our stages, without any additional charge for stage fare."

Auburn became the grand battleground for the rivals, for during the preceding decades, lines of stages had been placed upon the new and improved lateral roads leading north and south.

The "Old Line's" answer to the new adversary was the swift "Telegraph" coach, a conveyance limited to six passengers, manned by the most experienced and careful drivers and the best and fleetest teams. These stages traveled day and night with unqualified success.

The "Telegraph," "Eagle" and Pilot" runs were the pride of the road. Horses were changed every 10 miles and the average speed of these expresses was eight miles an hour.

The establishment of the Pioneer Line required much planning as evidenced by guidelines published in the *Rochester Observer* of March 14, 1828:

1. The duty of the commissioners is, to find proprietors, establish the general principles by which they are to be governed, and procure the pledge and countenance of the community to support the Line of their preference.

2. Each proprietor is to own as many miles of the line, as shall be agreed upon, and sustain the whole equipage and expenses, of that part of the route, there being no joint stock in the concern.

3. It is our intention, so far as practicable, to have carriages and harness entirely new, and horses first rate, for that business.

4. The drivers are to be men who do not swear nor drink arden spirits, and who prefer the house of public worship on the Sabbath, to the noisy bar-room.

5. We are happy to believe that some of our taverns will be without bars, and intend that every house where horses are changed, a supply of Hot Coffee shall always be in waiting, at a low price, to the passengers, and free to the drivers.

"It is hoped that the proposed Line may be established and in operation as soon as 1st June next, though it may not be practicable early.

"All we can further say definitely is, we feel deeply interested and intend to pursue with perserverance and energy, this object, to its perfect accomplishment; counting that we are understood by our brethren Commissions, and that we are to act as one man, 'being of one heart and one mind,' and counting on the progress of all who love our Lord Jesus Christ in sincerity of whatever name or denomination."

The Pioneer Line interests gained control of the Western Exchange Hotel, the best then in Auburn, and hoped by refusing to accommodate "Old Line" passengers, and by turning Colonel John M. Sherwood's horses from their stables into the streets, they'd steal the march on their rivals.

A few days, however, sufficed to fit up Eldad Steel's brick building across the street from the Western Exchange, as a hotel known as the Bank Coffee House. This became Sherwood's general headquarters and remained so until his American Hotel was opened in 1830.

Auburn residents did not remain quiet spectators of this tournament and came to the support of the Old Line in large and respectable numbers. A public meeting was held in the court yard in front of the court house on Saturday, August 23, 1828, at which a series of resolutions was adopted:

It was resolved that "all associations and combinations of men formed to prescribe and dictate to others in what manner they shall observe and keep the Sabbath are subversive of the free exercise of conscience; that the

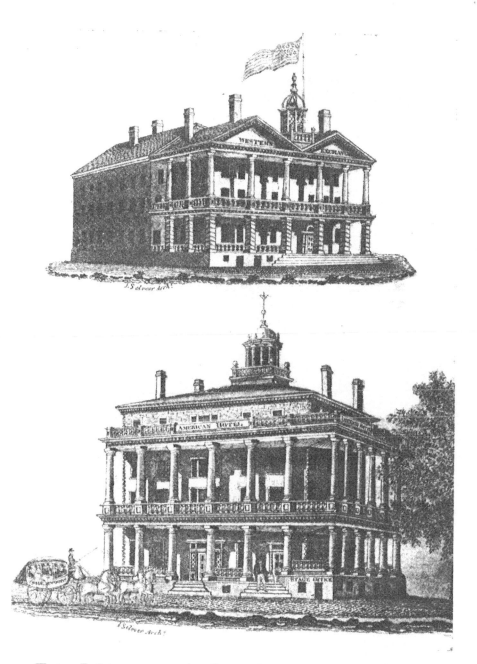

Western Exchange, top, catered to "Pioneer Line" traffic in Auburn. To compete, the Sherwood's built the elegant "American Hotel" across the street (below) in 1830. Both were famous hostelries in their day.

members of this meeting, hereby enter their solemn protest against the forming or organizing any religious party in politics."

These were much the sentiments of a religious newspaper published in Auburn called the *Gospel Advocate*. On September 13, 1828, it remarked:

> "The Pioneer line of stages, had it been started on the principles of fair competition, would have excited no emotions beyond the individuals concerned, but when it was established for a religious purpose and in tones of authority demanded the patronage of the religious part of the community, thus endeavoring to enlist the religious prejudices of society against individuals who have long been faithful servants of the publick, it excited the just reprobation of an insulted community."

The Pioneer Line was seen by the *Advocate* as "but a wheel in a vast machine, which is intended to ruin all individuals whatever their profession or pursuits who are orthodox in their faith."

Competition was, and still is, the life of business. The great stage war which would ensue for three years proved this. The "Telegraph line of stages outgoes even the speed promised by its proprietors when they started it," recorded the *Onondaga Register* on September 10, 1828. One stagecoach, it said, made the 296 miles between Buffalo and Albany in the "almost incredible" time of 45 hours and 14 minutes, including delays and stops.

It was a fight to the finish. Each line patronized its own taverns along the line. In one case, in the village of Waterloo, Pioneer Line stages rushed up to the Green Hotel, where they either discharged passengers for the night or stopped to change horses. Old Line stages frequented the nearby Eagle Tavern and Waterloo Hotel. Passengers received the very best in accommodations and it was not unusual to see four coaches in front of the Eagle, with as many as 50 people partaking of breakfast or dinner.

Although the Pioneer Line was well stocked with first class horses and fine new coaches, it employed inexperienced drivers. Fast driving was the consequence of competition, much to the advantage of the Old Line. For, in making fast time, good judgement in the management of horses must be exercised — when to drive fast, when to go slow, and when to drive moderately.

Also taken into consideration must be the care given to horses at the end of each run; in feeding, watering and exposure. The Pioneer enterprise was its own worst enemy in these respects. The result was that the Old Line drivers with long years of experience proved themselves in the strife. Although they were frequently subjected to racing with Pioneer stages, which were fully their equal, the latter soon had to contend with impaired horses.

This was the consequence of indiscretion in driving and want of care at the stables. It gave rise to a monstrous relay of horses, contributing greatly to the line's

The Eagle Tavern, opened in January, 1819, by Quartus Knight in Waterloo, as the "Waterloo Coffee House" was the stopping place for Pioneer Line stages during the "stage war." It burned down on January 24, 1869. (Photo courtesy Waterloo Library and Historical Society)

downfall. Old Line drivers were told to "load light and go behind" as the "Pioneer Line" drivers were prone to overload and overdrive.

News columns were often spiced with stories of hair-breadth escapes and Jehu-feats of the drivers. On one occasion an Old Line driver was discharged for racing with a Pioneer coach. Taking special note, the *Onondaga Register* on July 22, 1829, said:

> "On complaint of one of the proprietors of the Old Line of Stages, one of the drivers of that line was fined by Justice Kasson of this place the sum of $20.00 for driving his horses upon the run in the village of Geddes, on the 13th inst. Altho' in justification by the driver, it was shown that the racing was commenced by one of the Pioneer driver's attempting to pass him upon the run, yet, in this instance, this pernicious and dangerous practice has received its merited award. It is much to be lamented, that more frequent examples of this kind are not made to deter the thoughtless and imprudent drivers of placing the lives of their passengers in iminent danger.
>
> "But the promptness with which this offence has been punished, and that too on the complaint of one of the proprietors, gives assurance that at least their line of stages the safety of their passengers shall not be endangered by some foolish competition. Let stage proprietors pursue this worthy example, and stage accidents will be much less frequent. In addition of the penalty of 20 and costs, the driver was discharged by his employers."

Despite its assertions to the contrary, the Pioneer Line resorted to underselling its competitors by lowering its fares. This made it possible for almost anyone to ride their stages. On one occasion, two women were compelled to accompany seven drunk men from Canandaigua to Auburn, "whose deportment was disgusting." Later, the agent of the Pioneer Line in Geneva professed regret over the circumstance, promising it would be corrected.

It was quoted by the *Cayuga Patriot* of Auburn on April 1, 1829, that "Since the above case, two of the Pioneer passengers called into a grocery in this place, somewhat intoxicated, and procured their bottles filled with real raw whisky. On being questioned, one of them said he had paid but seven shillings for his passage from here to Rochester. Thus whilst the respectable traveller pays full fare, he is liable to be associated with a set of drunken black-guards, who pay almost nothing. This is Pioneerism! Religion connected with a money-making business! Holy stages, adorned with pictures of Angels, and drunken passengers belching forth profanity and lewdness. Can Religion gain by such an association?"

On another occasion, a Pioneer Line stage driver endeavored to force his desires on a female passenger, for refusing to gratify the brutal desires of himself and companions. He was arrested and faced court action in Rochester.

Colonel John M. Sherwood of Auburn, the powerful stagecoach magnate, had visions that his mighty empire would eventually crumble to the railroads in the wake of progress. His views were broad and elevated.

Sherwood's elegant home on the then outskirts of Auburn was a showplace. He became famous for the raising and breeding of pure-bred stock and was once president of the New York State Agricultural Society.

The struggle came to the attention of John Fowler, an English traveler, on a tour of New York State in 1830:

"Since leaving Albany, I had been frequently told, I suppose by those interested in supporting the old line of stages, that the new, or Pioneer line, had sold out their stock, and discontinued running. I had my suspicious as to the accuracy of the information, and at Geneva I found them fully confirmed, there being a meeting of the proprietors at the inn where we dined, at which it was resolved to carry on the most vigorous opposition, but I hate monopolies of all kinds; and as regards these stages, before there was a choice of conveyances, I have heard enough of the inconvenience which persons sustained in travelling just upon the terms which might be dictated to them; and once myself, when upon a cross road, where the old line had it all to themselves, besides breaking down, which, to be sure, might have occurred to either party, I had such a sample of their proceedings as I should not wish to experience again. We scarcely averaged more than three and a half miles an hour; and in urging the drivers even to that speed, had to submit to no little insolence into the bargain. When upon the main roads, where both lines have been plying, the state of things has been widely different — the fare moderate, speed nearly doubled, and a spirit of accommodation evinced by drivers and all connected with the establishment. I hope and trust the public will so far support the new line, as to warrant them in keeping the field. There is travelling enough for both, and the disposition to travel will keep pace with the facilities afforded. Where two concerns may thrive, and the public at the same time be much better accommodated, there can be no reason why one should engross its exclusive patronage, to confer upon it a small amount of benefit. 'Live and let live,' is a good old-fashioned maxim, not withstanding being somewhat outre in the present day. I wish both parties success, and a fair competition and understanding between them; but neither merely to oppose or subvert the other."

Picking up a newspaper of the day, one might read such a notice as:

"Stage fare reduced — Pioneer stages from Rochester and Utica, four dollars per seat and under; and to intermediate places in proportion. Caution to the Public. — A variety of methods having been reported to in order to impress the public mind with the belief that the Pioneer stages are discontinued, the public are respectfully informed that the proprietors of said line are running two daily lines of stages between Rochester, Canandaigua, and Utica, and one daily line from Utica to Albany, (sabbaths excepted;) and that in point of comfort, speed, and low rates of fare, this line shall not be surpassed."

Isaac Sherwood, like other stage proprietors, owned or controlled a number of inns. One of the most noted was the Sherwood Inn in Skaneateles, shown here before it was torn down in 1872. West wing of building is the original 1807-era Sherwood tavern. Present Sherwood Inn is not the original building, although on the same site. *(Photo courtesy Onondaga Historical Association)*

Shortly after the Pioneer Line was established, some $60,000 was raised through solicitations and contributions. Josiah Bissell of Rochester was the prime mover in the effort. "The Pioneer Line of stages must, will, and shall succeed," he proclaimed; "I will sacrifice every cent of my property to support it. If necessary, I will take the bread from my children's mouths for its support. It is on God's side and must prosper. Rather than see the hopes of God's people cloven down, I will write Reverend on the front of my hat, mount the Pioneer stage box, take the reins and drive the coach myself."

The scoffers howled in derision and the press of the day was filled with stories at the expense of the Pioneer Line. Among the more sarcastic items appearing in a newspaper was:

"Wanted. A good Orthodox family horse which

must not do work on the Christian Sabbath, and which will not need any meat or drink that day."

"Money Wanted. $10,000 on ample security at 6 percent, the interest to stop on Sunday. Orthodox money preferred."

Coming to the defense of the Pioneer Line, a contemporary observer commented that in one sense it was a failure and its advocates were heavy losers. "But the agitation of the subject which placed their comfortable and well managed coaches upon the road resulted in a great and lasting good. Public sentiment was educated to a higher regard for the Lord's Day; and although the extreme measures of the Sabbath party were defeated, it gained much for religion and true progress."

The Pioneer, in spite of its efforts to win the popular favor, lost prestige and gradually weakened. A grand combination of indignation, inexperience, and failure to secure the mail contracts resulted in its downfall.

The editor of the *Lyons Advertiser* said on September 3, 1830, that "These Pioneer lines were established, no doubt, by worthy, excellent men. But they saidly misjudged as to the best means of using money to do good."

The Pioneer Line continued in operation until 1831. Through the years, it was customary for stage lines to pay tolls for crossing Cayuga Bridge on a quarterly basis. Between 1828 and 1831 tolls collected from the Pioneer Line were but a fraction of those paid by the Old Line. The ledger book of the Cayuga Bridge Company in the Buffalo and Erie County Historical Society reveals:

Year	Sherwood's "Old Line"	Pioneer Line
1828	$1,587.75	$457.36
1829	$2,314.37	$957.47
1830	$2,375.32	$510.43
To 3/31/31	$ 390.97	$ 62.50

The Pioneer Line thus broke down and withdrew altogether, leaving the Old Line proprietors masters of the situation until the coming of the railroad. Isaac Sherwood later admitted to a friend in confidence that the Pioneer Line drove him hard, and if the siege had continued much longer, he would have been obliged to throw in the reins.

Chapter 13

Twilight Years

Although the 1830s were the most prosperous for the Old Line proprietors, with stage lines on all major roads, they realized the days of the stagecoach were numbered with the advent of railroads. For this reason, one is not surprised to find their names as officers, directors or stockholders in this new mode of transportation.

Railroading was in its infancy at the time, but it held great promise for the future. Colonel John M. Sherwood, the great stage proprietor of Auburn, liberally invested in the Auburn and Syracuse Railroad in 1836. Later, he was an officer in the Auburn and Rochester Railroad.

It was recorded that Sherwood "actually assisted in that consummation from a patriotic conviction that the interests of individuals must always, in a country like ours, give way before public requirements. His views were broad and elevated."

In December, 1837, Sherwood contracted to operate the Auburn and Syracuse Railroad with horses. Thomas Y. How, Jr., of Auburn, treasurer of the company, wrote to a stockholder on January 4, 1838:

"I am much pleased to be able to state that 22½ miles of the road is so far finished that we have made a contract with J. M. Sherwood the mail contractor to run that part of the road which is ready for use with horsepower until the first of July next — he giving us one half of the receipts from passengers and one half of the receipts from freight. Inasmuch as three miles of the road are not yet graded and will not be finished

129

until May or June next, we decided for our best interests to contract out the use of the road upon liberal terms to the stage proprietors so as to dispose of any competition with hem and turn the travel entirely over the road."

On Christmas Day, December 25, 1837, about 50 people boarded two passenger cars — a little larger than stagecoaches — for a ride over the completed portion of the line, about 13 miles. The horses, furnished by Sherwood, were changed about five miles east of Auburn. The railroad was officially opened to Geddes, near Syracuse, with an excursion on January 8, 1838. Five cars crowded with passengers were pulled by horses to near Syracuse, treated to dinner at the Syracuse House. They returned to Auburn that evening.

"My father's family was invited to one of the early trial trips," wrote Frederick W. Seward, son of William H. Seward, the famous statesman from Auburn. He said, "Mr. Sherwood, the stage proprietor, and his family, occupied the adjoining compartment in the one passenger car. Another was improvised by putting one of Sherwood's stages on a platform car. Thus equipped, and drawn by horses, we made the journey to Syracuse in what seemed the marvelously short time of two hours and a half."

Due to financial difficulties brought on by a tight money market, Sherwood operated the line for 19 months. Two horses in tandem usually drew two coaches over the wooden rails, each of which accommodated 24 persons. The trip took an average of three and a half hours; the horses being changed twice. The fare from Auburn to Syracuse was a dollar.

One of the shortcomings of the pioneer rail lines was the lack of cooperation between companies; a situation remedied early in the days of stagecoaching. In a letter to his friend, Governor William H. Seward, on December 29, 1839, Sherwood noted this lack of cooperation which resulted in much inconvenience to travelers. He noted each railroad had its own hours of arrival and departure and frequently, passengers and mail were delayed for a day because of uncoordinated timetables.

"Each company is desirous to run their own road for their particular interest without reference to the interest of other companies or the convenience of the traveling publick," Sherwood wrote, adding "the only way that I can see to remedy this evil is by Legislative enactment." This would regulate arrivals and departures of trains. He recommended the establishment of "through" service, the cost being borne proportionately by the several individual railroads, as had been done by stage proprietors for years.

Although Sherwood recognized this problem it did not become a major cause of concern until the completion of the Attica and Buffalo Railroad on November 24, 1842. This was the last link in the chain of railroads between Albany and Buffalo.

The changing of cars and baggage at Schenectady, Utica, Syracuse, Auburn, Rochester and Batavia caused public indignation as the railroads by now had become the favored mode of travel. Under a plan similarly outlined by Colonel Sherwood, the railroads established through service on June 1, 1843. This network of railroads across the state was consolidated under an act dated April 2, 1853, forming the New York Central Railroad.

With the advent of railroads, the old turnpikes took a turn for the worse, receiving a staggering blow because they took away their long-distance traffic. It had started with the canal, but the railroad was the straw that broke the camel's back. None of importance survived if they paralleled a railroad.

Shorter turnpikes, serving local traffic, especially those connecting farming communities with markets, survived into the 1840 and 1850s. Some endured for a few years longer as plank roads.

But generally, the original purpose of toll roads no longer existed, and were turned over to local communities for maintenance under the path master system. The state had grown sufficiently in population and taxes were now adequate for maintenance. Paying tolls was seen as a petty annoyance.

The "Old Line" ultimately withdrew, leaving lateral routes to the locals who employed dilapidated hacks unworthy of the name "stagecoach" to carry the mail to the rural post offices in areas yet unpenetrated by railroads.

Kellogg Tavern, Palmyra, N. Y. — Circa 1820s) *(Sketch by Walter Drury)*

Conclusion

"On one hand lay the Turnpike, where the Stages of Messrs. Thorp & Sprague, once the swiftest messengers of which we could boast, now seemed, in the comparison, to stand still!" So wrote a passenger aboard the first train on the Utica and Schenectady Railroad through the Mohawk Valley on July 25, 1836.

Travel was now at the parting of the ways. Stagecoaching would continue to exist but a few more years to link disconnected railroad lines. The old familiar advertisements for the "Telegraph," "Pilot," and "Eagle" lines disappeared from the newspapers of the day. In their stead appeared the railroad time schedules offering travelers transportation far superior to the jouncing coach.

By 1840, the "Old Line Mail" had been entirely supplanted by the railroads as far west as Auburn, although there were still a few stage proprietors still convinced they could compete with the steam locomotive. John Butterfield, still operating the remnant of Jason Parker's once-thriving stage business, established a daily line between Utica and Syracuse in January, 1840.

Since the trains operated primarily at night, the stages ran during daylight hours only, "and they intend to perform the distance in as good time as the cars, and occasionally beat them," said the editor of the *Oneida Whig* of January 7, 1840. He added, "we hope the enterprising proprietors will not be left by the travelling public to pocket the loss."

Staging enjoyed a brief revival in Albany in the fall of 1841 when the Mohawk and Hudson Railroad abandoned its incline plane track from the old depot on State

Street to the junction at the top of the hill, north of the capital.

A group of citizens organized a line of stages to compete with the railroad, and for a time it was a success. So many people rode the stage from Albany to Schenectady, it was said the old turnpike had not seen such use even in the palmiest days of staging.

On October 23, 1841, for instance, 27 stages went over the road, carrying an average of eight passengers at 50 cents apiece. During the first seven days of operation, 1,698 passengers were carried by the stagecoaches over this route. This only a brief Indian Summer existence, however.

Stagecoaches were taken off the road west of Auburn with the completion of the Auburn and Rochester Railroad in November, 1841, and by the following year the rail network was completed to Buffalo.

The stage proprietors themselves had not put their eggs all in one basket, and had been gradually shifting their efforts to new enterprises. Having an affinity with the old, they turned to steamboats, the railroad, express and telegraph companies; into which they poured the wealth garnered from the stage business.

The proprietors, superintendents and agents of the "Old Line" were a strong lot, enterprising and progressive. The early 19th century was not a time when great enterprise was the order of the day. A man to create and extend a new business then was considered visionary and rash.

Through the years, the Old Line had influence. The dear old Mohawk Bank, in its day of pride and solitary glory, had a feather in its cap to have the deposits of the Old Line. It had only one longer and gayer feather — the gilded patronage of the Literature Lottery, under the moral shield of Union College.

The stage barns now took a sympathetic lurch with the tottering business of the tavern. The departed stages left a somber mark on the old road. The long row of stalls where the horses had rattled their halter chains were now slips where hens hatched their broods. The stable-yard is a cemetery of broken coach bodies and wagons with iron work rusting away. Here, too, are the discarded fanning mills used to separate oats from chaff, and cutting boxes with single-knives set at guillotine slant, under which the heads of oat-sheaves had fallen into a basket, to be devoured by the horses.

Under a pile of chaff is a badly-worn curry comb. On the walls, collars, halters, and harnesses hang in cobwebbed disarray. The departed stagecoaches, in a sense, left a trail of decay and depression in their wake along the weed-grown turnpikes.

The business of the tavern dwindled and the steel pen grew rusty in the tumbler of birdshot. The landlord dozes in lonely wistfulness on the porch, the clatter of galloping horses and bleating stage-horn echo in his mind.

The tavern lights grow dimmer with the passage of time and the turnpike gate bangs with the wind dispassionately against he abandoned toll-house. What was an every-day way of life is now but a memory.

*   *   *   *   *

THE OLD TURNPIKE

We hear no more of the clanging hoof,
  And the stage-coach rattling by;
For the Steam King rules the traveled world
  And the old Pike's left to die.
The grass grows over the flinty path,
  And the stealthy daisies steal
Where once the stage-horse, day by day
  Lifted his iron heel.

No more the weary stager dreads
  The toll of the coming morn;
No more the bustling landlord runs
  At the sound of the echoing horn;
For the dust lies still upon the road,
  And the bright-eyed children play
Where once the clattering hoof and wheel
  Rattled along the way.

No more do we hear the cracking whip,
  Or the strong wheel's rumbling sound;
But ah! the water drives us on,
  And the iron horse is found!
The coach stands rusting in the yard,
  And the horse has sought the plow;
We have spanned the world with an iron rail,
And the Steam King rules us now.

The old turnpike is a pike no more,
  Wide open stands the gate;
We have made us a road for our horse to strain,
  When we ride at a flying rate;
We have filled the valleys, and leveled the hills,
  And tunneled the mountain side;
And round the rough crag's dizzy verge,
  Fearlessly now we ride.

On - on - on, with a haughty front!
  A puff, a shriek, and a bound;
While the tardy echoes wake too late,
  To babble back the sound;
And the old pike is left alone,
  And the stagers seek the plow;
We have circled the earth with an iron rail,
  And the Steam King rules us now!

Albany Argus, Jan. 3, 1840

Addendum

The following is from: *Autobiography of Thurlow Weed*, edited by Harriet A. Weed, Vol. 1, 1884. Houghton Miffiin & Co., publishers, pp. 140-156, Chapter XIV, 1824.

A Stage-Coach Accident. — First Meeting with William H. Seward. — Stage-Coach Traveling Half a Century Ago.

While walking in the street at Rochester one afternoon I observed an accident to a stage-coach, and went with others to proffer assistance. It proved to be but a slight mishap, and the party, which consisted of the families of Judge Elijah Miller, of Auburn, and Judge Seward, of Orange County, who were returning from Niagara, soon proceeded on their way. The casual meeting thus was the beginning of my acquaintance with William H. Seward. It grew rapidly on subsequent occasions, when he was called to Rochester on professional business. Our views on general politics were not dissimilar, and in regard to anti-masonry, he soon became imbued with my opinions.

Very few of our citizens possess information, other than traditional, of the mode of travel between Albany and the western part of New York, even as late as 1824. Those who step into a railway car at Albany at seven o'clock in the morning, and step out to get their dinner in Rochester at two o'clock, P.M., will find it difficult to believe that, within the memory of by no means the "oldest inhabitant," it required, in muddy seasons of the year, seven nights' and six days' constant traveling in stages to accomplish the same journey.

And yet that was my own experience in April, 1824.
We left Albany at eight o'clock in the evening, and traveled diligently for seven nights and six days. The road
from Albany to Schenectady, with the exception of two
or three miles, was in a horrible condition; and that west
of Schenectady, until we reached "Tripes" or "Tribes
Hill," still worse. For a few miles, in the vicinity of the
Palatine Church, there was a gravelly road, over which
the driver could raise to a trot; but this was a luxury experienced in but few localities, and those "far between."
Passengers walked, to ease the coach, several miles each
day and each night. Although they did not literally carry
rails on their shoulders, to pry the coach out of ruts, they
were frequently called upon to use rails for that purpose.
Such snail-paced movements and such discomforts in
travel would be regarded as unendurable now. And yet
passengers were patient, and some of them even cheerful,
under all those delays and annoyances. That, however,
was an exceptional passage. It was only when we had
"horrid bad" roads that stages "drew their slow lengths
along."

But stage-coach traveling had its bright as well as its
dark aspects. I will endeavor to reverse the scene. Take,
for illustration, an early September day. The coach leaves
Rochester after breakfast in the morning, if with a full
complement, nine passengers inside and two on the box
with the driver. At Pittsford and Mendon and Victor,
where the stage stops to change the mail and water the
horses, a lady or boy, but usually a lady, comes with a
basket of peaches, of which the passengers are invited to
partake, but for which they are not permitted to pay, except in thanks. At Canandaigua, a beautiful village, then
rejoicing in a greater number of distinguished men than
are now to be found in any interior city of our State, we
get dinner; and the dinners at "Blossom's," as all who
ate them will remember, were dinners indeed. To prove
what I say in relation to the distinguished residents of
Canandaigua, I will name Gideon and Francis Granger
(postmasters-general under Madison, in 1812, and Har-

rison, in 1840), Nathaniel W. Howell, John Greig, John
C. Spencer, Myron Holley, Oliver Phelps, Dudley Marvin, Henry B. Gibson, Jared Wilson, Mary H. Sibley, etc.;
two or three of whom are almost certain to become our
fellow passengers. Peter Townsend and Joseph Evering-
ham are highly intelligent young merchants from New
York city, who have lately established themselves there.
George H. Boughton, subsequently a state senator and
canal commissioner from Lockport, was then a merchant's clerk at Canandaigua. There were others, if not
wits themselves, the occasion of wit in others. To this
class *Spienceer Chopin*, who mawkishly affected the Scot-
tish accent, and Judge Atwater belonged. When a prisoner
was on trial for an attempt to break open Judge Atwater's mansion, the judge himself became a witness. His
manner was deliberate, and his language pedantic. He
stated that he was awakened at the "witching time" of
night by an unusual noise; that on listening attentively
he became satisfied that burglars were attempting to
enter his castle; that he assumed an erect position on his
bed, and at that particular moment "Bose" spoke. Dudley Marvin, the prisoners counsel, rose, and with quaint
solemnity said: "May it please the Court, I am not a little
surprised that the witness, himself an eminent jurist, who
on other occasions graces the seat which your Honor now
occupies, should so far forget the law of evidence and the
gravity of a charge which affects the liberty of my client,
as to proceed in this most irregular manner. No persons
knows better than my distinguished friend, Judge Atwater, that the testimony he is giving is wholly irregular.
If it is important that this court and jury should know
what 'Bose' saw and heard on the night of this alleged
burglary, Bose himself must take the witness's stand.
Bose is no stranger; we all know him as sagacious, observing, and vigilant." This produced an irresistible out-
break, involving the audience, the bar, the jury, and the
court, in roars of laughter. And when, after an interval of
several moments, order was attempted to be restored, it
was found quite impracticable to proceed, and the case

was actually laughed out of court. Here we find as fellow-passengers, Mr. Wadsworth or Major Spencer, of Geneseo, Mr. Ellicott or Mr. Evans, of Batavia, Mr. Coit, Major J. G. Camp, or R. B. Heacock, of Buffalo, General Porter, of Black Rock, General Paine, of Ohio, and others, who arrived in the stage from Buffalo.

Leaving Canandaigua, we are driven through a charming series of agricultural landscapes to Geneva, sixteen miles, where we have a view of its beautiful lake, a lake not unlike or unworthy of its equally beautiful namesake in Switzerland. At Geneva either Joseph Fellows, a land agent, Henry Dwight, a banker, or Mr. Prouty, a marchant, is pretty sure to join us. From Geneva to Waterloo, four miles, seems but a turn of the kaleidoscope, and the distance from Waterloo to Seneca Falls is gotten over in no time. At Seneca Falls the chances are at least one to two that we are joined by Colonel Mynderse, who is going over to Auburn to visit his friend, Judge Miller.

The drive over Cayuga Bridge, more than a mile in length, was always pleasurable and interesting. Some one would remark how much it was to be regretted that a lake so large should be of so litle practical value, not being used for purposes of navigation or inhabited by fish of any value.[1] Looking north, we discern the Montezuma marshes, where Comfort Tyler failed to manufacture salt; while a southerly view, though you do not actually see, directs your attention to the beautiful village of Aurora, near the head of the lake, then the residence of Jethro Wood,[2] Humphrey Howland, Ebenezer Burnham, Ephraim Marsh, etc., and now of the Morgans, wealthy and reputable merchants; also of William H. Bogart, the veteran senate reporter, and the "Sentinel" letter-writer of the New York "Courier and Enquirer" and New York "World," a gentleman who has been for more than thirty years about the legislature without becoming obnoxious

---

[1] Cayuga Lake is now inhabited by excellent fish, and navigated by steam and canal boats.

[2] The inventor of the iron plow.

to charges of improperly interfering with legislation. Here, too, resides in palatial splendor Henry Wells, who, more than thirty-five years ago, "solitary and alone," with a single carpet-bag, founded and inaugurated what is now the American Merchants' Union Express Company. I first knew Mr. Wells more than forty years ago, teaching boys "how not" to stutter. My only son was one of his pupils. But though Mr. Wells cured others, he could not cure himself. Mr. Wells still lives to enjoy the fruits of his prosperity, and may he live long and happily, for I have known few men more worthy of prosperity. A few miles from Aurora, beautifully situated upon the lake shore, is a valuable farm, purchased many years ago by Moses H. Grinnell, one of the merchant princes of the city of New York, for some relatives, who reside there.

When finally over the long bridge, we discuss Thomas Mumford, a lawyer residing at the end of it, and Colonel Goodwin, a worthy tavern-keeper, midway between Cayuga Bridge and Auburn. And during the many years that I was accustomed to travel in stages between Cayuga and Auburn, I cannot remember the time that some of the passengers did not amuse the coach by relating an incident that occurred to Mr. John C. Spencer several years before. The coach drove up to the hotel at the end of the bridge, to water the horses. It was a dark, rainy, cold evening. The stage was full inside and out. A lady, closely veiled, came to the steps, who was, as the keeper of the hotel said, very anxious, on account of sickness in the family where she resided, to get to Goodwin's that evening. The passengers said it was impossible, as there were already nine of them inside. But Mr. Spencer, prompted by his sympathies or his politeness, as it was but four miles, thought a lady ought not to be refused a passage, and offered, if she chose to accept it, a seat on his lap. The offer was accepted, the lady took her seat, and the stage dashed off. At Goodwin's Tavern, where the lady got out, a light was brought to enable her to find a part of her luggage, and when she removed her veil, a very ebony colored individual of the feminine gender was revealed, to the consternation of Mr. Spencer, and the amusement of the other passengers!

At Auburn we rest for the night, having made sixty-four miles. In the evening, the magnates of the village drop into the hotel bar-room to gossip with the stage passengers. There were no sitting or drawing rooms at hotels in those days; nor could a single lodging room, or even single bed, be obtained. In country inns, a traveler who objected to a stranger as a bedfellow was regarded as unreasonably fastidious. Nothing was more common, after a passenger had retired, than to be awakened by the landlord, who appeared with a tallow candle, showing a stranger into your bed!

The leading men of Auburn were Judge Miller, George B. and E. S. Throop (since governor), Nathaniel Garrow, Parliament Bronson, etc. William H. Seward had commenced his professional and public life at Auburn one year before. Genial "Kit" Morgan was at Yale College.

In the morning, the stage was off between daylight and sunrise. The passengers refreshed themselves, enjoyed a view of refreshed and invigoratd nature, to which the rising sun soon began to impart light and life. The canal was attracting business and population; the stage had just begun to run over the Northern or New Turnpike, leaving the villages of Skaneateles, Marcellus, Onondaga, West Hill, Onondaga Hollow, and Jamesville, on the line of the old turnpike, to a process of decay which has rendered them almost obsolete. I ought to have remarked that, at Auburn, passengers always dreaded an acquisition to their number in the person of Mr. Wood, who, weighing some four hundred pounds, and inconveniently broad across the shoulders and transom, made the coach every way uncomfortable. As a sleeper and snorer, he would compare favorably with any one of "the seven." For ten or fifteen miles there was litle of outside interest to talk about. In passing through Camillus, the richly cultivated farms and large granaries of the brothers Squire, David and Nathan Munro, attracted attention, and some one would be pretty sure to remark that "the Munros not only owned the best farms in the town themselves, but had mortgages on all their neighbors' farms," which was true. Our approach to stage-houses and post-offices was announced by the blowing of a tin horn or trumpet, with more or less skill, by the driver. This drew together a crowd of idlers, with this difference between New York and many parts of Europe, — that instead of beleaguering the coach with imploring appeals for charity, our visitors would generally present us with some choice fruit.

At Syracuse, twenty-five miles from Auburn, we breakfasted. Syracuse then, as now, was a marvel in the suddenness and rapidity of growth. And here, *my* story came in. I had worked in the Onondaga furnace in 1811 and 1812, and remembered having gone through what was now the flourishing village of Syracuse, with six or seven hundred inhabitants, when it was a tangled and almost impenetrable swamp, thickly inhabited by frogs and water-snakes. Indeed, the swamp foliage was so thick, and darkened the atmosphere to such an extent, that the owls, mistaking day for night, could be heard hooting. Upon the locality over which the now large and beautiful city of Syracuse has extended, there was, in 1811, but one human habitation; that was Cossett's Tavern, on the site of the present Empire House. At the western boundary of the swamp, on the creek which empties into the lake, there was a small grist-mill and two log-cabins. In September, 1812, soon after the declaration of war with England, a letter was written by the Secretary of the Navy (Dr. Eustis), showing how lamentably that cabinet minister's geographical education had been neglected. Captain Woolsey, who commanded the United States brig, Oneida, was ordered to proceed from Oswego to Onondaga, there to take on board the cannon ball manufactured at the Onondaga furnace for the government.[1]

---

[1] This is paralleled by the supply of tanks for *holding fresh water,* sent from England for the English vessels of war built at Kingston during the War of 1812.

And this incident reminds me of another, and one which at this day will be regarded almost as incredible as the order of the Secretary of the Navy; for, while ships were unable to ascend the rifts and falls of the Oswego River, salmon did make their way from Lake Ontario through the Oswego River and the Onondaga Lake into the Onondaga Creek, and were killed two miles south of the city of Syracuse. I remember well of being attracted, in the spring of 1811, to Wood's mill-dam by torches flitting below the dam in the creek. Arriving at the spot, I saw Onondaga Indians with clubs watching for and killing salmon, as they were seen making their way over the rifts. I joined in the sport and came out with a fine salmon as my share of the spoils. I carried my salmon to Mr. Joshua Forman (then a lawyer in Onondaga Hollow, subsequently the inventor and father of Syracuse), for which he paid me a large, round, bright silver dollar; this being my exact recollection of a coin which was of more value to me then, and was a source of higher gratification, than the receipt of thousands of dollars in after years. I then spoke of Judge Asa Danforth, indicating his residence in the Hollow, who was the first white inhabitant of Onondaga County. This led me to speak of Ephraim Webster, a white boy found among the Onondaga Indians, after the Revolutionary War in the Mohawk Valley. Young Webster, as he grew up, like Joseph among the Egyptians, grew in favor with the Indians. Before white inhabitants reached that part of the State, young Webster had been made a chief of the Onondaga nation, and had married a daughter of an Indian, and received as her bridal portion a mile square of lands belonging to the Onondaga nation. Mr. Webster continued to reside with his Indian wife and the tribe long after the county was organized and settled by white inhabitants. In 1808 or 1809, Governor Tompkins appointed Mr. Webster agent of the State, to receive and disburse the money paid annually to the Onondaga nation. He was subsequently appointed a Justice of the Peace and Judge of the County Court. After the death of his Indian wife, in 1810 or 1811, he married an intelligent and reputable white lady, with whom he was living happily when I last heard of him, with children by both wives growing up in harmony and affection. Mr. Webster was a man of good sense, good habits, and good character, enjoying alike the respect and confidence of his white and red neighbors and acquaintances.

After breakfast, we leave Syracuse and drive rapidly on to Manlius Square, where passengers were always warmly welcomed at the stage-house by its host, Colonel Elijah Phillips, one of nine brothers, all men of mark, of whom I shall have occasion to speak hereafter. Mrs. Phillips, an estimable lady, was the granddaughter of Judge Danforth, and the first white child born in the county of Onondaga. Manlius was the residence of Azariah Smith, a merchant remarkable for his enterprise, activity, industry, and integrity. He had a greater and more varied capacity for business than any other man I have ever known. He was many years supervisor of the town, doing not only his own business thoroughly, but the business of almost every member of the Board of Supervisors. As a member of the legislature, his time and talents were severely taxed. Though chairman of the Committee on Claims, and a member of two or three other working committees, while discharging all their duties promptly, he found leisure and was always ready to do the work of fifteen or twenty idle or incompetent members from other counties. He was also an administrator or executor of such of his neighbors as left property requiring attention.

If, as the horn blew for passengers to take their seats, John Meeker did not, at the last moment, make his appearance, some one would express surprise at his absence. John Meeker was an extraordinary man. He owned and cultivated three or four of the largest farms in the towns of Pompey, Tully, and Preble. He had stores, not only in those three towns, but in Fabius, Homer, and Manlius, managed under his personal supervision by clerks. He always sold produce at the lowest prices for cash, or on approved credit. He paid the highest prices in cash or goods for black salts, and for pot and pearl ashes. He had an ashery as an appendage to each of his stores. He went frequently to Albany and New York to purchase goods. He was an uneducated man, with the appearance and in the costume of a common farmer. With all these establishments, spreading over so large a surface, it will be apparent that Mr. Meeker was a man of extraordinary business talents; but when people have so many irons in the fire, some of them will inevitably burn, while others as inevitably get cold; and in the end, like many others who over-trade, John Meeker "came to grief."

In passing near the town of Pompey, Pompey Hill would be suggested as the residence of Henry Seymour, a capable canal commissioner (and father of ex-Governor Horatio Seymour). Victor Birdsye, an eminent lawyer and equally eminent statesman, also resided at Pompey Hill. There, too, Samuel S. Baldwin, a flash lawyer and fast gentleman, resided. He married Juliana, a daughter of Judge Peter W. Yates, who enjoyed a waxwork celebrity in Trowbridge's Museum as the "Albany beauty." Judge Yates, when, in the early years of the present century, he resided at Albany, occupied, if he did not erect, the mansion subsequently owned by James Kane, and successively occupied by Governors Tompkins, Clinton, and Seward.

From Manlius we passed through Eagle Village to Canaseraga Hollow, where the chances were in favor of picking up General J. J. M. Hurd, of Cazenovia, a merchant with agreeable manners, who went to Albany and New York to purchase goods as often as was convenient, he evidently fancying that part of his business. In ascending a hill, eastward, the stage stops at the suggestion of some passenger, who invites the others to go with him a few rods from the road and look at an immense petrified tree, lying upon the surface, and perfect, except where it had been broken to gratify the curiosity of visitors, each of whom, of course, carried away a specimen. A few miles further east brought us to Quality Hill, where passengers always promised themselves enjoyment at the expense of a most polite, obsequious, and good-natured tavern-keeper. Mr. Webb (for that was his name) was truly an original. In deportment, if he had lived in London, and been a dancing-master, instead of keeping a hotel on Quality Hill, he might have rivaled Turveydrop; in his zeal to preserve the credit of his house, and his tact in concealing the meagerness of his larder, Caleb Balderstone might have taken lessons with advantage from our host of Quality Hill. Here, in all probability, one of the numerous family of Spencers would be added to our list of passengers, among the survivors of whom I know only Mr. Julius Spencer, a most worthy man and an essential fixture in the Albany office of the New York Central Railroad. Proceeding eastward, and after rising Breakneck Hill, we came to the Oneida Castle, the residence of the Oneida tribe of Indians. These Indians, long surrounded by white inhabitants, had emerged from their savage habits and customs, and were enjoying the advantages of civilization. These advantages consisted of loafing about taverns and groceries and in drinking bad whiskey. Full two thirds of the tribe had ceased to hunt, or to fish, or to cultivate their lands, than which none more fertile were to be found in the State. Large numbers of both sexes were idling about the tavern, all or nearly all of them endeavoring to sell some trinket for the purpose of buying whiskey. This process of demoralization went on until the few who did not die prematurely were induced to emigrate to Wisconsin. After leaving the Castle, the passengrs would talk of the devotion of Rev. Mr. Kirkland to the Oneida Indians, of the eloquence of Skenando, one of their aged chiefs, and of a French officer, Colonel de Ferrier, who married an Indian wife at Oneida Castle, and whose sons and daughters were well educated ladies and gentlemen; and this topic would scarcely be exhausted when we were driven into the village of Vernon, where we always changed horses.

In Vernon itself there was was nothing especially remarkable. The hotel was kept by a Mr. Stuart, whose sons and grandsons were persons of more or less consideration in different parts of the State for many years afterward. From Vernon to Westmoreland was but a few miles. The hotel at Westmoreland was kept by Mrs. Cary, a widow lady with six or seven attractive and accomplished daughters, who, as far as propriety allowed, made the hotel pleasant for its guests. These young ladies, quite well known by intelligent and gentlemanly stage passengers, were sometimes irreverently designated as "Mother Cary's chickens." In this, however, no disrespect was intended, for, though chatty and agreeable, they were deservedly esteemed, and all, "in the course of human events," were advantageously married.

From Westmoreland we were driven rapidly through New Hartford into Utica, seventy-two miles from Auburn. This was the end of our second day's journey. But, for the accommodation of those who preferred a night ride, a stage left Utica at nine P.M. Those to whom time was important took the night line. We, however, will remain over. Utica is now no "pent-up" place. But as, in an earlier part of this narrative, I have given a brief account of its highly intelligent citizens, we will pass on. And departing early the next morning, the first object that attracts the attention is the pleasantly-situated mansion and fruitful surroundings of Colonel Walker, an aide-de-camp of General Washington in the Revolutionary War. A few miles farther on, as we cross the Mohawk River, the humble farmhouse pointed out is the residence of Major-General Widrig, who was ordered, with his division, into the service during the War of 1812. But that major-general was found to be so lamentably defficient in penmanship, orthography, and arithmetic as to render his resignation as proper as it proved acceptable. Farther on, in the town of Schuyler, I pointed to a lofty, two-pronged pine tree, under which, in September, 1814, the regiment to which I belonged, commanded by Colonel Mathew Myers, of Herkimer, ate its first ration; and where, to my great satisfaction and as grateful remembrance, the quartermaster of the regiment, George Petrie, then a merchant, subsequently a member of Congress, and now a venerable clerk in the General Post Office at

Washington, appointed me his quartermaster's sergeant.

Before reaching the ancient village of Herkimer, we were driven over the fertile, and celebrated German Flats, nearly a thousand acres of which were owned by Judge Jacob Weaver and Colonel Christopher Bellinger. They were neighbors, and, unless drawn into political discussion, warm friends. During a sharply contested election in the spring of 1814, while at the polls, these old gentlemen collided. The conversation waxed warmer and warmer, until they were about to engage in a personal conflict. Friends, however, interfered in season to avert what both in their cooler moments would have lamented. Subsequently they shook hands and calmly reviewed their cause of quarrel. "You ought not," said Colonel Bellinger, "to have lost your temper." "And you ought not," said Judge Weaver, "to have called me a British Tory." "I only did so," said Colonel Bellinger, "after you called me a French Jacobin." "And then," said Judge Weaver, "you not only called me a British Tory again, but said that I rejoiced when Oxenburgh was taken, and I couldn't stand that." Many amusing anecdotes were told of Judge Weaver's early life, when he was a merchant and trading with the Indians. In purchasing furs, as the story goes, his hand, placed on the scale opposite the fur, weighed half a pound, and his foot a pound. His accounts were kept on boards, in chalk. One of his neighbors, Mr. Harter, in settling an account found himself charged with a cheese. Being a farmer, and making not only cheese for his own table, but cheese he was in the habit of selling at the store, he asked an explanation. Judge Weaver, priding himself upon his accuracy, was impatient with all who disputed his accounts. But Mr. Harter appealed to his reason and common sense to show how improbable, if not impossible it was, that he who made cheese for sale should have been a purchaser. This perplexed the judge, who, after thinking and talking for a long time, was unwilling under the circumstances, to press his neighbor to pay for a cheese, and equally unwilling to admit an inaccuracy

in his bookkeeping. The question was finally laid over
till the next day, in the hope that the judge might be able
to verify the integrity of his books, or boards. On the following day, when Mr. Harter appeared, the judge met
him in jubilant spirits, exclaiming, "It is all right; I remember all about it now." "But," said his neighbor, "you
don't mean to say that I bought the cheese!" "No, no,"
said the merchant; "it was not a cheese, but a grindstone;
and I forgot to put the hole in it!" In Judge Weaver's
mode of bookkeeping, a circular chalk-mark represented
a cheese, while the same mark, with a dot in the centre,
converted it into a grindstone. Those two splendid farms
have long since, by a very common process, been melted
into one. General Christopher P. Bellinger married the
daughter of Judge Weaver, and thus inherited both
farms. General Bellinger, a very worthy man, with whom
I served in the legislature of 1830, and who has been for
fifty-seven years my intimate friend, is still living. Here
resided also Major Weber, a wealthy German farmer,
who was with us at Sackett's Harbor. Though a second
officer in our regiment, he found the service anything but
pleasant. I have an order now in my possession, directing
me to take possession of a building for a regimental hospital, no word of which with more than two syllables is
spelt right, and which is signed, "J. P. Weber, Coma-
dand." On one occasion, when Sir James Yeo's fleet appeared off Sackett's Harbor, for the purpose, as was supposed, of landing troops, and our regiment, with others,
was ordered to a point directly opposite the fleet, Major
Weber was in a greatly excited state, constantly asking
subordinates and privates if they supposed the British
intended to land, and complaining of the injustice of
pushing militia instead of regular troops into such an exposed position. It was not, he said, on his own account
that he was unwilling to be crowded into battle where he
was sure to be killed, but on account of the feelings of his
wife, who was in delicate health. He inquired also whether
he couldn't resign his commission. Fortunately, however,

for the major, after a couple of hours of trepidation and suspense the fleet made sail and soon disappeared.

From Herkimer to Little Falls, seven miles, there were no particular attractions; nor indeed was there much of interest at the Falls, a small village, with a valuable water-power, nearly unavailable on account of its being owned by Mr. Edward Ellice, a non-resident Englishman. Mr. Ellice was a large landholder in this State and in Canada. It was my privilege, in 1861 and 1862, to become well acquainted with him in London. He enjoyed the reputation of being the most influential commoner in England. He was a man of giant frame and intellect. He was one of the oldest members of Parliament, and had been once or twice a member of the British Cabinet. He died at his country-seat in Scotland in 1864, in the eighty-third year of his age. The London residence of Mr. Ellice, in Arlington Street, looking into St. James's Park, now improved and modernized, was occupied by Horace Walpole a century ago, and in it many of his celebrated letters were written.

From Little Falls we come after an hour's ride to a hill, by the bank of the river, which several years before General Scott was descending in a stage, when the driver discovered, at a sharp turn near the bottom of the hill, a Pennsylvania wagon winding its way up diagonally. The driver saw but one escape from a disastrous collision, and that, to most persons, would have appeared even more dangerous than the collision. The driver, however, having no time for reflection, instantly guided his team over the precipice and into the river, from which the horses, passengers, coach, and driver were safely extricated. The passengers, following General Scott's example, made the driver a handsome present as a reward for his courage and sagacity. We dine at East Canada Creek, where the stage-house, kept by Mr. Couch, was always to be relied on for excellent ham and eggs, and fresh brook trout. Nothing of especial interest until we reach Spraker's, a well-known tavern that neither stages nor vehicles

of any description were ever known to pass. Of Mr.
Spraker, senior, innumerable anecdotes were told. He was
a man without education, but possessed strong good
sense, considerable conversational powers, and much natural humor. Most of the stories told about him are so
Joe-Millerish that I will repeat but one of them. On one
occasion he had a misunderstanding with a neighbor,
which provoked both to say hard things of each other.
Mr. Spraker, having received a verbal hot shot from his
antagonist, reflected a few moments and replied, "Fergu-
son, dare are worse men in hell dan you," adding, after
a pause, "but dey are chained." Mr. Spraker used to say
that when his son David was a boy, he thought he would
make a smart man; but he sent him to college, and when
he came back from Schenectady, he didn't know enough
to earn his living.

At Canajoharie a tall, handsome man, with graceful
manners, is added to our list of passengers. This is the
Hon. Alfred Conkling, who in 1820 was elected to Congress from this district, and who has just been appointed
judge of the United States District Court for the Northern District of New York by Mr. Adams. Judge Conkling
is now (in 1870) the oldest surviving New York member
of Congress. The late Hon. Samuel R. Betts, recently
United States Judge for the Southern District of New
York, was elected to Congress from Orange County in
1815. John Cramer, of Saratoga, though the senior of
Judge Conkling, being over ninety, was not elected to
Congress until 1833.

In passing Conine's Hotel, near the Nose, the fate of
a beautiful young lady, who "loved not wisely, but too
well," with an exciting trial for breach of promise, etc.,
would be related. Still farther east, we stop at Failing's
tavern to water. Though but an ordinary tavern in the
summer season, all travelers cherish a pleasant remembrance of its winter fare; for leaving a cold stage with
chilled limbs, if not frozen ears, you were sure to find in
Failing's bar and dining rooms "rousing fires;" and the

remembrance of the light, lively, "hot and hot" buckwheat cakes, and the unimpeachable sausage, would renew the appetite even if you had just risen from a hearty meal.

Going some miles farther east, we come in sight of a building on the south side of the Mohawk River, and near its brink, the peculiar architecture of which attracts attention. This was formerly Charles Kane's store, or rather the store of the brothers Kane, five of whom were distinguished merchants in the early years of the present century. They were all gentlemen of education, commanding in person, accomplished and refined in manners and associations. Charles Kane resided in Schenectady, James Kane in Albany, Oliver Kane in New York, Elias Kane in Philadelphia, and Archibald Kane in the West Indies. An incident which occurred there in 1808 is remembered by some of the passengers, who relates it. Some gentlemen, who had been invited to dine there, amused themselves after dinner with cards. In the course of the evening a dispute arose between Oliver Kane and James Wadsworth, of Geneseo, a gentleman of high intelligence, great wealth, and enlightened philanthropy, the latter years of whose life were distinguished for zeal and liberality in the cause of normal schools and school district libraries. The quarrel resulted in a challenge, and the parties met before sunrise the next morning, under a tall pine tree, on a bluff behind the store, and exchanged shots, Mr. Kane receiving a slight wound. More than thirty years afterward, I was walking with Mr. Wadsworth and his son, the late General J. S. Wadsworth, in Broadway, where he met Mr. Oliver Kane, with whom young Mr. Wadsworth exchanged salutations; and observing that his father passed making "no sign," he said, "Don't you know Mr. Kane?" "I met him once," was the laconic reply. Supposing that James had not heard of the duel, when we were alone I mentioned it to him, to which he replied, laughing, "I knew all about that, but I wanted to draw the governor out." I had endeavored, several years earlier, to induce Mr. Wadsworth to accept a nomination for governor, and thereafter James S. was accustomed to speak to and of him as Governor.

Here Commodore Charles Morris, one of the most gallant of our naval officers, who in 1812 distinguished himself on board the United States frigate Constitution in her engagement with the British frigate Guerriere, passed his boyhood. In 1841, when I visited him on board of the United States seventy-four-gunship Franklin, lying off Annapolis, he informed me that among his earliest recollections was the launching and sailing of miniature ships on the Mohawk River. On the opposite side of the river, in the town of Florida, is the residence of Dr. Alexander Sheldon, for twelve years a member of the legislature from Montgomery County, serving six years as Speaker of the House of Assembly. The last year Dr. Sheldon was in the legislature, one of his sons, Milton Sheldon, was also a member from Monroe County. Another son, Smith Sheldon, who was educated for a drygoods merchant, drifted some years ago to the city of New York and is now the head of the extensive publishing house of Sheldon & Co., Broadway.

The next points of attraction were of much historical interest. Sir William and Guy Johnson built spacious and showy mansions a few miles west of the village of Amsterdam, long before the Revolution, in passing which interesting anecdotes, relating to the English baronet's connection with the Indians, were remembered. A few miles west of Sir William Johnson's, old stagers would look for an addition to our number of passengers, in the person of Daniel Cady, a very eminent lawyer, who resided at Johnstown, and for more than fifty years was constantly passing to and from Albany. At Amsterdam, Marcus T. Reynolds, then a rising young lawyer of that village, often took his seat in the stage, and was a most companionable traveler. He subsequently removed to Albany, where for more than a quarter of a century he held a high professional and social position.

And now, as the valley of the Mohawk spreads out more broadly, and the eye wanders over fields teeming with the bountiful products of Mother Earth, we come in view of Schenectady, first seen by a graduate of Union, who immediately comes eloquent in his laudation of Dr. Nott, whose sermon at Albany against duelling, occasioned by the death of General Hamilton, is claimed as the greatest effort of the age. Our graduate would then enumerate the distinguished men scattered over the Union who owed their success in life to Dr. Nott's peculiar mode of lectures and training. Then, as we approached the old bridge across the Mohawk he would tell us how long it had withstood storm and tempest, and how many dark secrets it would disclose if it could talk. Next, he would have a brief history of Mr. Givens, the gentlemanly keeper of the hotel in Schenectady, and of his still more gentlemanly son, Major Givens, who brought back from West Point to Schenectady all the discipline and proprieties, physical and social, of a military education, and who vibrated for half a century between Schenectady and Saratoga, saying and doing polite and civil things to and for everybody. Perhaps allusion might be made to Mr. Given's predecessor in the hotel, only for the purpose of remarking that his daughter, a beautiful and accomplished loung lady, rejected wealthy suitors for the sake of the fine person and melodious voice of a music master, preferring, it would seem, musical to circulating notes; concluding, almost certainly, with an account of a phrenological discussion, in which Governor Yates floored his antagonist by saying, "My head is not so long as Governor Clinton's, but it is a great deal *ticker*."

From Schenectady to Albany, the drive through dwarf pines and a barren soil, the turnpike road ornamented with poplar trees at uniform distances on either side, was tame, and, unless enlivened by conversation, dull. But it was an unusual circumstance to find a stage-coach, with fair weather and good roads, between Rochester and Albany, that was not enlivened by conversation, for there were almost always two or three intellectual passengers. Myron Holley, for example, with a gifted and highly-cultivated mind, had committed to memory, and would recite by the hour, gems from the British poets. Mr. Granger also had a good memory, and would often, during the evening, recite from Burns, Moore, and others. Richard L. Smith, a lawyer from Auburn, with his wit and drolleries would make hours and miles seem short. And there was an unfailing source of fun at every stopping-place in the "gibes and jokes" of the stage-drivers, who, as a class, were as peculiar, quaint, and racy as those represented by the senior and junior Weller in "Pickwick," as Samivel described them, — a class of highly-social individuals, who have been driven off the roads and compelled to earn a precarious living by tending pikes and switches, or marrying "vidders," and whose unintellectual successors are engine-drivers and stokers.

The stage-drivers of that day lived merry but short lives. The exceptions were in favor of those who, after a few years' experience, married some reputable farmer's daughter on their route, and changed their occupation from stage-driving to farming. This must, I think, have been the case with one of my earliest stage-driving acquaintances. It is but a few weeks since I saw in the papers the announcement of the death, somewhere in Tompkins County, of Phineas Mapes, aged eighty years. "Phin Mapes," a rollicking stage-driver at Catskill, is one of my earliest remembrances. In 1803 or 1804, a stage with four live horses was an institution, at least in the admiring eyes of boys. I remember with what a flourish Mapes used to dash up to the post-office door, and, while Dr. Croswell was assorting the mail, how gracefully and gently he would throw his long whip-lash over the backs of the leaders, and how, by the responsive action of their fore-feet, nostrils, and ears, they would show how well they understood that he meant it playfully. How well, too, I remember when, in 1810 or 1811, I renewed my acquaintance with this driver at Skaneateles, between which place and Onondaga Hollow he was blowing his horn and cracking his whip and his jokes, quite as popular here as he had been at Catskill. The oldest inhabitants of Catskill and Skaneateles, as well as the few survivors who rode in stages upon the great Genesee turnpike sixty years ago, will remember Phin Mapes pleasantly, from whom, in his best days, Dickens might have found a "jolly" original for Mark Tapley.

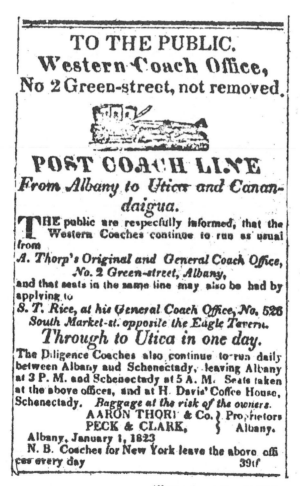

TO THE PUBLIC.
Western Coach Office,
No 2 Green-street, not removed.

POST COACH LINE
From Albany to Utica and Canandaigua.

THE public are respecfully informed, that the Western Coaches continue to run as usual from

A. Thorp's Original and General Coach Office,
No. 2 Green-street, Albany,

and that seats in the same line may also be had by applying to

S. T. Rice, at his General Coach Office, No. 526
South Market-st. opposite the Eagle Tavern.

Through to Utica in one day.

The Diligence Coaches also continue to run daily between Albany and Schenectady, leaving Albany at 3 P. M. and Schenectady at 5 A. M. Seats taken at the above offices, and at H. Davis' Coffee House, Schenectady. *Baggage at the risk of the owners.*

AARON THORP & Co. ⎫ Proprietors
PECK & CLARK, ⎬ Albany.

Albany, January 1, 1823

N. B. Coaches for New York leave the above offices every day   39tf

Albany Argus, Jan. 7, 1823

Appendix II

The Cherry Valley Turnpike

(From the Cazenovia, N. Y. *Republican,* Feb. 23, 1859)

The abandonment of the Turnpike from Cherry Valley to Manlius, and the dissolution of its Company, is an event of sufficient local interest to deserve a notice in our country papers; and a brief glance at its history may be worth the attention of those who live on properties which once derived much of their value from the advantage which it afforded, and who remember many of its earlier managers as pioneers in the improvement of Central New York.

True, in these days, when travellers deem any speed less than thirty or forty miles an hour cause for complaint; when railroads are built annually for hundreds of miles; when almost any speculator talks of millions more glibly than our fathers did of the hundreds of thousands which they earned with such slow labor and husbanded so carefully — the construction of a simple wagon road, seventy miles in length, may seem an affair of small importance. It was not so regarded, however, ten years after the settlement of this country, when railroads were not dreamed of, steamboats were far in the future, and even the Erie Canal (though in some form contemplated by a few far-sighted men) was generally considered a visionary project. The "Great West" was then a great waste, of which even the Government knew little; the lakes above Niagara were hardly navigated at all; the Indians had possession, full, quiet, and peaceable so far as they pleased, of all, except a few points in Kentucky and Ohio and a few military posts along the rivers of the West and Northwest.

Western New York was then the region attracting emigration, as Iowa and Wisconsin are now; the opening of a new route of travel to it parallel with the Mohawk was a considerable enterprise; and its originators, when they had obtained a capital of nearly one hundred thousand dollars, payable in great part in labor, to construct this turnpike, westward from the old revolutionary frontier settlement of Cherry Valley, felt as much elated as a modern company which has raised in stock and borrowed on bonds half a dozen millions to stretch an iron road across the State.

The title given to the road, "The Third Great Western Turnpike," may seem grandiloquent to us—but appeared very just to them, for it was in their estimation indeed a "great" affair.

The charter was passed by the legislature of 1803, and the first organization was made November 16th of that year, when the electors met at the house of Ebenezer Hale, in Sangerfield, and elected John Lincklaen, president, Samuel Sidney Breese, secretary, and James Green, treasurer.

Ashael Jackson, well remembered as an old citizen of Nelson, and Samuel Clemmons were appointed to explore a route for the road. It was agreed to make arrangements with the Oneida Turnpike Company (whose road extended from Cazenovia by Peterboro to Vermon) for the joint use of that part of their road forming what is now Albany street in Cazenovia.

On Nov. 14, 1804, a third meeting was held (also at Mr. Hale's, in Sangerfield), when the first election of directors was held. The persons chosen were John Lincklaen, Benjamin Gilbert, Ashael Jackson, John Diell, Calvin Smith, Aaron Morse, Oliver Norton, Samuel Clemmons, James Green, James Morse, Samuel Sidney Breese, Samuel St. Clair, and Robert Wilson.

Benjamin Gilbert and Samuel Clemmons were made a committee to put the road under contract, at a total cost not to exceed the capital of the company (then $75,000, but afterwards increased to $95,000).

At a meeting held at the house of Ebenezer Johnson, in Cazenovia, April 9, 1805, it was voted that stockholders might pay the greater part of their subscriptions in labor in constructing the road, also that additional stock should be issued; and at a meeting, 4th February, 1806, 15,000 of stock was appropriated to be expended under the direction of John Diell, Benjamin Gilbert and Calvin Smith, in making the first ten miles of the road west from Cherry Valley. This ten miles of road appears to have been the first section completed. It was accepted, and a resolution passed directing a gate to be built on it, August 4, 1808. The bridge over the west branch of the Unadilla was contracted to be built by Samuel Rindge, for $500, February 7, 1809. The greater part of the road appears to have been completed in December, 1809, as three more gates, including the one west of Cazenovia, were then ordered to be built.

At a meeting held at the house of Uri Beach, in Sangerfield, August 6, 1810, all the seven gates were finally located. It was voted that wagons with tires more than six inches broad might pass free of toll. On the 26th December, 1811, the first dividend was declared being $12½ per share.

Later dividends were advertised in the *Cherry Valley Gazette* and *Cazenovia Pilot*.

The business of the road, thus fairly began, increased and became very large. The main westward emigration passed over it and the rival route by the Mohawk, and with the white-covered emigrant wagons went westward, others, drawn by powerful teams, carrying all the goods sold in this part of the State. On the other hand, the produce of the counties along the line of the road, and much of Western New York, then just being opened to settlers, was carried over it to the eastern markets. During both summer and winter droves of cattle paced constantly over it; loads of grain, barrelled beef and pork, potash and other products of the fields and forests, went rolling on wheels or sliding on sleighs along its line; and through its wooded avenues and sunny clearings, over its log causeways and newly-graded hills, past its new wooden houses and log-cabins, there was a constant stream of busy life and travel.

During the war of 1812-'15, the temporary check to emigrant travel was compensated by the employment on the part of government of many teams in the transportation of munitions of war to Generals Brown and Scott and their men, fighting on the Niagara frontier.

The scarcity of specie during the latter part of the war was a source of much annoyance to the toll-gatherers, and on the 7th October, 1815, the Company resolved to issue as their contribution to the abundant "shinplaster currency" of the day, a thousand dollars worth of tickets, varying in denomination from three to fifty cents.

This three penny necessity, however, was obviated by great events elsewhere, as a note in the Secretary's handwriting states that — "N.B. Peace between Great Britain and the United States took place, and it was thought unnecessary to have the tickets printed."

Our older residents yet remember when there was a public house at every mile or two on the road, where the traveller would see teams resting under the shed, and teamsters smoking at every door; and we have heard it said, that the odor of the tar with which the wheels were lubricated could be perceived in the air in still weather from here to Albany. Among the innkeepers of more or less note along the road during its busy days, we may mention, at Manlius, Phillips, Fox and Dwight; at Buelville, Hale; at Oran, Loomis and Bartholomew; west of the Cazenovia Lake, Philemon Tuttle; at Cazenovia, Ebenezer Johnson, Mclean, "Captain" E. S. Jackson, "Sheriff" Whipple, Daniel Day, Jesse Kilborn; at Togg Hill, Hitchcock and Coolidge; east of Nelson, near "Buck's," Ira Clark; at Morrisville, Farwell and Bick-

Typical among the inns on the old Cherry Valley Turnpike was this one built at Sangerfield in 1793 by a Colonel Norton, who came from Connecticut. It is said members of the Loomis Gang attended parties here. It is now an antique shop owned by William Seward Allison.

nell; east of Morrisville, were Abiather Gates, on the hill, Peleg Brown at its eastern foot, and Lelands at Pine Woods; at Madison, St. Clair, Goodwin, Burton and Turner; at or near Sangerfield, Montgomery, Norton, Hale, Beach and Rindge; at Bridgewater, Curtis, Bostwick and Page; at Winfield, Martin, Prendergast and Crowell; at Richfield, Carver, Dr. Hatch, Richards, Coates, Benedict and Burgess; at Warren, Tunnicliff and Averill; at Springfield, "Capt." Coats, Cook, Scollard and Heyes; at Cherry Valley, Fitch, Walton, Sanders and Storey.

Nearly all the inns were good, but there were some, such as Goodwin's at Madison, Prendergast's at Winfield, Hatch's at Richfield, Averill's and William Storey's at C. Valley, and several others, which had a wide reputation. The traveller, driving (as was then so constantly done) in his own conveyance to or from Albany, often took pains so to regulate his journey as to reach one of these houses at night; and though they boasted little of elegance, he found in their blazing fires, clean rooms, well spread tables, a degree of comfort and substantial enjoyment not now easily found in the highly expensive and splendid hotels through which the flood of modern travel pours and roars.

During these years of prosperity, the Company made dividends of two and a half or three per cent, semi-annually; and in 1816, the dividends of the year amounted to seven per cent, so that stock was considered a good property. — But with the opening of the Erie Canal there came a change, for the heavy freighting soon left the wagons and took to the boats; and the valley of the Mohawk assumed that leading rank as a route of commerce and travel which it has never lost and seems destined to maintain permanently.

The route over the hills by Cherry Valley and Cazenovia, however, continued to have a share of stage-coach travel, as well as a large amount of business from private conveyances; and the breadth of the road (six rods) as well as the fact that it was by about thirteen miles the shortest route from Syracuse to Albany, rendered it long a favorite route for the cattle which wended their slow way, "on the hoof" from western pastures to the market of Albany or Boston; the stockholders still realized dividends amounting to about one and half per cent, semi-annually, and the farmers had an abundant market for hay and corn, and a profitable demand for yard-lodgings for cattle and swine. — But with the introduction of railroads, the passenger travel rapidly declined. The last distinct injurious effect from the railroads was when they began to carry livestock as freight, and soon took all the drives from the road.

But even after this, the dimuniation of the business and income went on. A new set of routes came into existence about ten years since, at the era of plank roads, on the easy grades and smooth surfaces of which the business of Central New York was drawn more and more every year into north and south channels to the railroads, the east and west highways were deserted.

The revenue of the road dwindled rapidly, and though it has outlived most of its contemporary turnpikes, it has

for years been evident that it could not long sustain itself.
The last dividend of three-fifths per cent, was paid from
the earnings of 1856, and the stockholders have now for-
mally relinquished their property to the road districts.
The road has done its part, such as it was, in the useful
development of the country, and yields to the more effi-
cient means which have been supplied by the invention
and energy of later generations. Something of it yet remains as a legacy to the country; seventy miles of broad
right-of-way acquired at its expense; many thousand
loads of stone and gravel spread along its bed; a considerable amount of grading; and bridges, causeways, and
embankments of no small cost in the aggregate. When we
mention the stone bridge built at a cost of over $500 and
yet perfect, each of Nelson; the bridge on Albany street,
built but a few years since; the heavy embankment (cost
$800) on Forman street, and the causeway at the foot of
the Lake; it will be seen that this district certainly has
gained some permanent and useful advantages from the
old road.

Probably the road even in its present inferior state of
repairs, may fairly represent one third or one half of its
capital, certainly could not be replaced for less, were its
route now in its original condition. This consideration
may deserve a moment's thought from some who habitu-
ally grumble on a turnpike and who, in their own objec-
tions to payment of the immediate sixpence demanded
at the gate, which to some seems only a legal form of
"highway robbery," may forget that to make and maintain the road, such as it has been, ninety-five thousand
good dollars or hard day's works were expended by the
last generation, who received but little interest on the in-
vestment which has at last proved a "dead loss" to their
successors. In all this, our local turnpike has been no exception to the general rule, for the capital spent in such
enterprises has generally been entirely sunk.

The fluctuations in the business of the road are worthy
of a little detailed notice, as giving indications of the
general course of business and travel in Central New
York.

The tolls, which in 1813 were $9,633, rose in 1815 to their highest point, $12,322. They declined by 1818 to $10,750, and in the hard times of 1820 and 1821, averaged only about $7,300. In 1822 they increased to about $9,500, after which came the permanent falling off caused by the Erie Canal. The receipts were in 1823 $8,382, in 1824, $5,079, in 1825, $4,920.

They oscillated between this sum and $4,420 for 23 years, except that (probably from the extensive westward emigration in wagons) they ranged in 1833, 1834 and 1835 from $5,100 to $5,700.

About 1848, new causes of depression occurred. The railroads began to carry freight, taking the droves from the road; and plank roads were introduced. Of these, many were constructed leading northward to the great railroad route, which thus concentrated almost all business and travel.

The result of this may be seen in the following statement:

Tolls received in	1848	$4712
” ” ”	1849	4498
” ” ”	1850	4084
” ” ”	1851	3252
” ” ”	1852	2578
” ” ”	1853	2348
” ” ”	1854	2034
” ” ”	1855	1721
” ” ”	1856	1623
” ” ”	1857	1305

Such an income being evidently insufficient to keep in good repair seventy miles of road, and there being no reason to expect an improvement, the company at their semi-annual meeting early last September, took measures to secure the consent of the owners of the road to its abandonment. This having been obtained, the gates were ordered open at the annual meeting of the 1st inst., and as soon as the unsettled business of the company can be adjusted, it will be entirely dissolved.

The dividends of the Company, during the fifty years since the first gate was erected, have been just three per cent per annum, on an average.

We may add a brief list of the citizens longest connected with the enterprise. Their "terms of office" were longer than is fashionable in these days of "rotation," and probably longer than they would have been, if their recompense either in cash or influence had been worth striving for.

Lincklaen, the first president, resigned after 18 years service, and was succeeded by Jonathan D. Ledyard, who after 36 years more, terminates his connection with the road at its discontinuance. The senior of the living directors is Major S. S. Forman, who has been a director for fifty years, and was secretary about thirty.

Hon. David H. Little, of Cherry Valley, was twenty-five years in the board, where his father, Dr. Little, had been for fifteen years before. Mr. Loring Down, of Mayflower, Otsego County, whose father, Col. Aaron Down, was a director for twenty-five years, has been director and superintendent of the road since 1834. Mr. Alexander White of Madison, in like manner succeeded his father, Mr. John White (who had been 19 years director), in 1835, and has since been superintendent of the western half. Mr. Archibald Bates, of Nelson, whose father was director for thirty years, has been in the board for thirteen more.

Of those not now living, the late Gen. Erastus Cleveland, of Madison, was a director for 41 years after 1806; Mr. R. G. Phelps, of Manlius, for 23 years; Dr. William Campbell, of Cherry Valley (well remembered as the old Surveyor General) for 30 years, from 1815 to 1845; Mr. James McCartney, of Madison, for 22 years, from 1824 to 1846. Others who were for considerable periods connected with the road, some of whom are still living, are Perry G. Childs, Charles Stebbins, Sidney T. Fairchild, J. Denise Ledyard, Ledyard Lincklaen, of Cazenovia; E. Clough and John McCartney, of Madison; Elias Montgomery, of Sangerfield; David Rindge of Bridgewater; J. Martin Prendergast, of Winfield; Josiah Bacon, of Waterville; James Arton, of Springfield; and Henry J. Campbell of Cherry Valley.

The enumeration may be of little interest to some of the younger or more recent residents of the line of the road, but to older inhabitants, not a few of these names will recall many reminiscences of "old times." To a very considerable extent the children of the oldest persons we have mentioned, are still residents on their paternal farms though many have done as their fathers did before them, sought newer regions, and devoted their energies to build up homes, towns, and society in remote States, which, when the now quiet villages on the "Cherry Valley Turnpike" were growing into their first importance, were buried in forests or formed parts of prairies untrodden by the foot of the white man.

*   *   *   *   *

Today, the Cherry Valley Turnpike is Routes 92 and 20 from Manlius to Cherry Valley. The portion (about 56 miles) from Cherry Valley to Albany was known as the "First Great Western Turnpike."

Preceding the New York State Thruway, Route 20 across New York State was widened and great stretches, particularly east of Cazenovia, were made a four-lane divided highway; as it was seen as the main east-west artery.

Today, however, the road has a new lease on life as travelers, wearied by monotonous Interstate Highways, again take to the more scenic old roads. Modern automobiles and trucks now roll along at 55 miles an hour where horses plodded along days on end covering the same distance now traveled in two or three hours.

Many of the old taverns still stand; many as country homes, and a number now being used as antique shops. The small village of Madison alone has 14 such shops.

The use of the term "Cherry Valley Turnpike" west of Cazenovia is a misconception that came into vogue primarily for promotional purposes, as there was no direct road westward from there until many years later.

NEW DAILY LINE OF

POST COACHES

From NEW-YORK to BUFFALO, by the way of ITHACA *and* GENEVA.

THIS line will leave New-York every day, Sundays excepted, and run thro' Newark, Springfield, Bottle Hill, Morristown, Succasunny Plains, Newton, Milford and Dundaff, *three times a week* by the way of Chenango Point, and *three times a week* by the way of Montrose, to Owego; and from thence daily, by the way of Ithaca and Ovid to Geneva, where it intersects a daily line to Rochester, Buffalo, Lewiston, &c. RETURNING—will leave Geneva at the same times and pursue the same routes to New-York. At Mott's, N. Milford, this line intersects the Newburgh line, which runs from thence, three times a week, to Newburgh.

The importance of this line to the public, will readily be seen: It opens a direct communication between the city of N. York and the western part of the state, thro' New Jersey and the northern section of Pennsylvania. At Newton (N. J.) it intersects a line which has recently been established from that place to Philadelphia, 3 times a week. At Montrose it intersects the line to Wilkesbarre, Harrisburgh, &c. At Chenango Point it intersects a line which runs north thro' Greene, Oxford, &c. to Utica, and intersects the Albany line, by Cooperstown and Cherry Valley, at Sherburne. At Owego it intersects a line which runs thro' Tioga Point, Elmira, &c. to Bath. Thus affording an opportunity to gentlemen who are wishing to travel in either of those directions, a cheap and expeditious mode of conveyance. The accommodations are good the distance less, and the fare much lower, than on any other route from New York to Geneva.

Good horses and coaches, and careful attentive drivers are engaged, and every attention will be paid by the Proprietors to the comfort and safety of Passengers.

☞ *Seats* may be taken at J. Patten's, 71 Cortland street, New York; at I. I. Roy's, Jersey City; Dawle's Tavern, Newark; at the Hotel, Dundaff; Buckingham's, Montrose; Robinson's Hotel, Chenango Point; either of the public houses in Owego; Ithaca Hotel, and at Grant's Coffee House, Ithaca; and at Faulkner's Hotel, Geneva.

S. HEMENWAY,   I. I. ROY,
ISAAC POST,   I. MOTT, & OTHERS.
January 1, 1825.   24

Geneva Gazette, **April 1, 1825**

Credits

The history of the stagecoach era in Upstate New York is a topic on which little has been written. Consequently, much research was done involving a host of individuals and organizations. I am indebted especially to the following for their efforts in assisting me:

Arnold Barben of the Seneca Falls Historical Society, John Genung of the Waterloo Library and Historical Society, Mr. and Mrs. Richard N. Wright and Violet Hosler of the Onondaga Historical Association.

The staffs of the following organizations generously availed me of local histories, newspapers and other pertinent historical information not readily available:

Buffalo and Erie County Historical Society; Cayuga County Historian's Office, Auburn; Cherry Valley Historical Society; Geneva Historical Society; Hobart and William Smith Colleges Library, Geneva; King's Daughters Library, Palmyra; Olin Library, Cornell University, Ithaca; Oneida Historical Society, Utica; Ontario County Historical Society, Canandaigua; Rochester Public Library History Department; Seward Mansion, Auburn; Seymour Library, Auburn; Syracuse Public Library Local History Department; Utica Public Library history room; Wayne County Historical Society, Lyons.

Also used extensively were the library and archives of the New York State Historical Association in Cooperstown, and the manuscripts division of the New York State Library in Albany.

Horse Boat Ferry.

THE subscribers having, during the last summer, finished and put into operation a

HORSE BOAT,

on Cayuga Lake—now give notice that the said BOAT will constantly ply, for the purpose of ferrying across the said Lake, from the termination of the 'Fifth Great Western Turnpike Road" n Genoa, to Kidder's old Landing in Ovid. The Boat will be kept in good order, and at all times will be furnished, with good horses and experienced hands. The distance across the said Lake is nearly three miles, which the Boat will perform in from twenty to forty minutes, in all reasonable times. The Boat is sufficiently large and convenient for ferrying eight waggons and twenty horses at a load. The distance from Albany via Cherry-Valley, Sherury and Homer, is 160 miles, and from Albany to Cayuga Bridge via Utica, is 178 miles—and it is presumed that the turnpike to this ferry is even better than any other great road leading into the western country. Persons travelling from the east to Bath, Angelica, Lake Erie, New-Connecticut, &c. &c. will find it for their interest to cross at this ferry. The rates of toll are the same as have been established and taken for eighteen years past, with said Boats.

JAMES KIDDER,
MATTHEW N. TILLOTSON,
DAVID OGDEN.

Cayuga Lake, Jan. 1st, 1819.   52 tf.

Cayuga Republican, July 14, 1819

Bibliography

Auburn and Syracuse Railroad, Treasurer's Letterbook, Syracuse University Archives.

Bagg, Moses, *Pioneers of Utica*, 1877.

Barclay, Captain, *Agricultural Tour in the United States and Canada*, London, 1842.

Bigelow, Timothy, *Journal of a Tour to Niagara Falls in 1805*, Boston, 1876.

Butler, Frances Anne, *Her Journal*, 1835, Vol. 11.

Clinton, DeWitt, *Private Canal Journal*, Albany, 1810.

Conkling, Roscoe P. and Margaret B., *The Butterfield Overland Mail, 1857-1869*, 1947.

DeWitt, Benjamin, *A Sketch of the Turnpike Roads in the State of New York* in Vol. 2, Transactions of the Society for the Promotion of the Useful Arts, Albany, 1807.

Duncan, John M., *Travels Through Part of the United States and Canada in 1818 and 1819*, London, 1823.

Earle, Alice Morse, *Stagecoach and Tavern Days*, New York, 1900.

Eddy, Edward Strutt, *Journal of a Residence and Tour in the United States of North America*, 1835.

Fowler, John, *Journal of a Tour of the United States in the Year 1830*, London, 1831.

Grant, J. Lewis, *Early Modes of Travel and Transportation*, Cayuga County Historical Society Collections Number Seven 1889.

Grip, *Historical Souvenir of Lyons*, 1904.

Hall, Captain Basil, *Forty Etchings from Sketches Made with a Camera Lucida, in North America, in 1827 and 1828*, London, 1830.

Hibernicus, *Letters of the Natural History and Internal Resources of the State of New York*, Letter XX, Canandaigua, June, 1820, pp. 93-94.

Holmes, Oliver Wendell, *The Stagecoach Business in the Hudson Valley*, Journal of the New York State Historical Association, Vol. 12, 1930.

Janson, Charles W., *The Stranger in America*, 1807.

Jones, Pomeroy, *Semi-Centennial of the City of Utica*, 1882.

Kingman, LeRoy W., *Early Owego*, 1907.

Laws of New York State, 1790-1840.

Leslie, E. Norman, *History of Skaneateles*, N. Y. 1902.

Leslie, E. Norman, *History of Skaneateles and Vicinity, 1781-1881*, Auburn, 1881.

Levasseur, A., *LaFayette in America, in 1824-1825*, Paris, 1829, Vol. 11.

Liancourt, Duek De La Rochefoucault, *Travels Through the United States ... 1795-1797*, London, 1800, Vol. 1, pp. 270-271.

Maxon, Norman, *The Genesee Pike*, Syracuse Herald article, Sept. 1, 1886.

McIntosh, W. H., *History of Ontario County, N. Y.*, Philadelphia, 1876.

McKeon, *Turnpikes* Manuscript, Onondaga Historical Association.

Miller, Elijah, *The Early History of Cayuga County*, mss. ca. 1835.

Munsell, Joel, *Annals of Albany*, various volumes.

New York State Agricultural Society *Annual Meeting*, 1872, Senate Document No. 95.

Nicholas, G. N., *The Rose Nicholas Trip from Virginia to New York State*, mss. Geneva Historical Society.

O'Callahan, E. B., *Documentary History of the State of New York*, Albany, 1850.

Tucker, Louis L., *Our Travels, A Knickerbocker Tour of New York State,
1822*, New York State Library, Albany, 1968.
Parsons, Irsael, *Centennial History of the Town of Marcellus*, 1878.
Phelps, Oliver C., *Phelps Family in America*, (2 vols.) 1899.
Postmaster General Records, Letterbooks, National Archives, Washington,
D. C.
Roberts, G. S., *Old Schenectady*, 1904.
"Junius," *St. Catherine's A to Z*, 1856. The St. Catherine's and Lincoln Historical Society, St. Catherines, Ontario, Canada, 1967.
Seneca Road Company *Memorial of, Relative to Railroad incorporations between Utica and Syracuse, and Auburn and Canandaigua, February 3, 1835*,
Assembly Document 148.
Spafford, Horatio Gates, *Gazetteer of the State of New York, 1824*.
Spafford, Horatio Gates, *Pocket Guide for the Tourist and Traveler Along the
Line of the Canals*, 1824 edition.
Spafford, Horatio Gates, *Some Cursory Observations on the Construction of
Wheel-Carriages*, Albany, 1815.
Stevens, Frank Walker, *Beginnings of the New York Central Railroad*, New
York, 1926.
Stimson, Hiram K., *From the Stage Coach to the Pulpit*, 1874.
Trollope, Frances, *Domestic Manners of Americans*, London, 1832.
Twining, Thomas, *Travels in America 100 Years Ago*, 1890.
Watson, Elkanah, *Men and Times of the Revolution*, 1856.
Weise, James Arthur, *Troy's One Hundred Years, 1789-1889*, Troy, 1891.
Welch, Samuel M., *Recollections of Buffalo during the decade from 1830 to
1840*, 1891.
Weld, Isaac, *Travels Through the States of North America and Provinces of
Upper and Lower Canada in 1795, 1796 and 1797*, Vol. 1, London, 1799.
Werthman, Francis, of Santa Barbara, California, *Correspondence*, (Utica,
N. Y., historian).
Whitford, Noble E., *History of the Canal System of the State of New York*,
1906, Vol. 1.
Woodworth, John, *Reminiscences of Troy*. 1860.

NEWSPAPERS

Advocate of the People, Auburn, New York.
Albany Argus, Albany, New York.
Albany Gazette, Albany, New York.
Cayuga Patriot, Cayuga Republican, Auburn, New York.
Dansville Village Chronicle, Dansville, New York.
Ithaca Journal, Ithaca, New York.
Lyons Advertiser, Lyons, New York.
Onondaga Register, Onondaga Hollow, New York.
Ontario Repository, Canandaigua, New York.
Rochester Daily Union, Rochester, New York.
Rochester Telegraph, Rochester, New York.
Skaneateles Press, Skaneateles, New York.
Western Repository, Canandaigua, New York.
Whitestown Gazette, Utica, New York.

THE "OLD LINE MAIL"
Stagecoach Days in Upstate New York

by RICHARD F. PALMER

The stagecoach era existed in Upstate New York for a half-century. From 1790 to 1840 the stagecoach reigned supreme as the mode of public conveyance. And during this period, the stagecoach proprietors on the great western routes aligned, or associated themselves; working in close agreement to control the road.

This syndicate, as it might be termed, was known as the "Old Line Mail" and during its existence it forced opposition after opposition off the road which attempted to gain footing!

Thorpe & Sprague controlled the Albany end of the business. Jason Parker & Co. carried on through Utica and westward, while Isaac and John M. Sherwood operated from Manlius to Canandaigua. The link to Buffalo and Niagara Falls was completed by Chauncey H. and Bela D. Coe, and others.

Although many hardships were encountered in traveling by stage, such a journey was not entirely void of pleasures. There were deep dark forests of towering hemlocks and pines. Here and there a little clearing appeared where a settler had built a log house, feebly attempting to cultivate the rutted soil.

The scenery was varied and interesting. The passengers were sociable, and many a warm and lasting friendship was formed in the old coach. Such was the way things were before the railroads.

About the Author ...

"OLD LINE MAIL" grew from Richard Palmer's interest in tracing old turnpikes and photographing houses that were once wayside taverns between Albany and Buffalo. A native of Palmyra, N. Y. (where his ancestors settled in 1810), he has always maintained an avid interest in local history.

As a reporter/writer for the *Syracuse Herald-Journal, Herald-American,* he particularly enjoys researching and chronicling different avenues of history usually neglected by the mainstream of historians.

"Many authors, particularly since the Bicentennial, tend to merely rewrite old history books and repeat old mistakes, rather than do fresh research and dig out new and little-known facts," Mr. Palmer said, adding, "'OLD LINE MAIL' is an example of fresh research."

He said: "Up to now, the great stagecoach days have only received passive mention in local histories. As I continued my research, I became more and more fascinated with the subject, especially since stagecoaching was such a big business in the early days. I felt that, after 150 years, its story needed to be told."